Genius: A Very Short Introduction

VERY SHORT INTRODUCTIONS are for anyone wanting a stimulating and accessible way in to a new subject. They are written by experts, and have been published in more than 25 languages worldwide.

The series began in 1995, and now represents a wide variety of topics in history, philosophy, religion, science, and the humanities. The VSI Library now contains over 200 volumes—a Very Short Introduction to everything from ancient Egypt and Indian philosophy to conceptual art and cosmology—and will continue to grow to a library of around 300 titles.

## Very Short Introductions available now:

Available soon:

For more information visit our web site
www.oup.co.uk/general/vsi/

Andrew Robinson

# GENIUS
## A Very Short Introduction

OXFORD
UNIVERSITY PRESS

# OXFORD
UNIVERSITY PRESS

Great Clarendon Street, Oxford OX2 6DP

Oxford University Press is a department of the University of Oxford.
It furthers the University's objective of excellence in research, scholarship,
and education by publishing worldwide in

Oxford New York

Auckland Cape Town Dar es Salaam Hong Kong Karachi
Kuala Lumpur Madrid Melbourne Mexico City Nairobi
New Delhi Shanghai Taipei Toronto

With offices in

Argentina Austria Brazil Chile Czech Republic France Greece
Guatemala Hungary Italy Japan Poland Portugal Singapore
South Korea Switzerland Thailand Turkey Ukraine Vietnam

Oxford is a registered trade mark of Oxford University Press
in the UK and in certain other countries

Published in the United States
by Oxford University Press Inc., New York

British Library Cataloguing in Publication Data
Data available

Library of Congress Cataloging in Publication Data
Data available

Typeset by SPI Publisher Services, Pondicherry, India
Printed and bound by
CPI Group (UK) Ltd, Croydon, CR0 4YY

ISBN: 978-0-19-959440-5

# Contents

# Acknowledgements

My interest in exceptional creativity began with writing a biography of Satyajit Ray in the 1980s. Though best known as one of the greatest of film directors, Ray was also a gifted and successful designer and illustrator, music and song composer, novelist and critic. Personal contact with him over several years showed me that genius, though everywhere rare, is a reality not an illusion. After Ray, I wrote biographies of other figures often regarded as geniuses: the physicist Albert Einstein, the poet and writer Rabindranath Tagore, the linguist and decipherer Michael Ventris, and the polymath Thomas Young. These eventually led to a study of exceptional creativity in the arts and sciences, *Sudden Genius? The Gradual Path to Creative Breakthroughs*.

In writing this brief introduction to genius – the first of its kind, so far as I am aware – I am grateful to several anonymous reviewers of the outline and manuscript, arranged by the publisher. Their comments both broadened the book's range, as befits its subject, and focused its approach.

It is a pleasure to thank Luciana O'Flaherty, Emma Marchant, Latha Menon, and Deborah Protheroe of Oxford University Press for their various contributions to the book.

# List of illustrations

# Chapter 1
# Defining genius

Homer, Leonardo da Vinci, Shakespeare, Mozart, and Tolstoy;
Galileo, Newton, Darwin, Curie, and Einstein. What do these
world-famous figures in the arts and sciences have in common?
– apart from the fact that their achievements are a century or
more old. Most of us would probably answer something like this:
all ten individuals through their work permanently changed
the way that humanity perceived the world: each possessed
something we call genius. But pressed to be more precise, we find
it remarkably hard to define genius, especially among individuals
of our own time.

Despite his fame and influence, Pablo Picasso's stature as a genius
is still debated, for example, as is that of Virginia Woolf in
literature. In science, Stephen Hawking, although often regarded
by the general public as a contemporary genius comparable with
Einstein, is not accepted as such by the physicists who fully
understand his work; they regard Hawking as only one of several
current luminaries in the field of cosmology.

Genius is highly individual and unique, of course, yet it shares a
compelling, inevitable quality – for the general public and
professionals alike. Darwin's ideas are still required reading for
every working biologist; they continue to generate fresh thinking
and experiments around the world. So do Einstein's theories

among physicists. Shakespeare's plays and Mozart's melodies and harmonies continue to move people in languages and cultures far removed from their native England and Austria. Contemporary 'geniuses' may come and go, but the idea of genius will not let go of us. Genius is the name we give to a quality of work that transcends fashion, fame, and reputation: the opposite of a period piece. Somehow, genius abolishes both the time and the place of its origin.

The word *genius* has its roots in Roman antiquity; in Latin, *genius* described the tutelary (guardian) spirit of a person, place, institution, and so on, which linked these to the forces of fate and the rhythms of time. Like the Greek *daimon*, the Roman *genius* followed a man from cradle to grave, as expressed in the poet Horace's lines from the 1st century BC defining genius as: 'the companion which rules the star of our birth, the god of human nature, mortal for each individual, varying in countenance, white and black'. Only genius knows, says Horace, why two brothers can differ entirely in personality and lifestyle. But *genius* among the Romans had no necessary relationship with ability or exceptional creativity.

Not until the Enlightenment did genius acquire its distinctly different, chief modern meaning: an individual who demonstrates exceptional intellectual or creative powers, whether inborn or acquired (or both). Homer, despite two millennia of veneration as a divinely inspired poet, did not become a 'genius' until the 18th century. This later usage derives from the Latin *ingenium* (not from *genius*), meaning 'natural disposition', 'innate ability', or 'talent'. It was already in wide currency in 1711, when Joseph Addison published an article on 'Genius' in his newly established journal *The Spectator*. 'There is no character more frequently given to a writer than that of being a genius', wrote Addison.

I have heard many a little sonneteer called a fine genius. There is not a heroic scribbler in the nation that has not his admirers who think him a great genius; and as for your smatterers in tragedy, there is scarce a man among them who is not cried up by one or other for a prodigious genius.

In the middle of the 18th century, Samuel Johnson attempted a definition in his periodical *The Rambler*, which is recognizably modern in its emphasis on genius as being something achievable through dedication. According to Johnson:

…[S]ince a genius, whatever it be, is like fire in the flint, only to be produced by collision with a proper subject, it is the business of every man to try whether his faculties may not happily cooperate with his desires, and since they whose proficiency he admires, knew their own force only by the event, he needs but engage in the same undertaking, with equal spirit, and may reasonably hope for equal success.

Not long after, Johnson's friend, the painter Joshua Reynolds, noted in his *Discourses on Art* that: 'The highest ambition of every Artist is to be thought a man of Genius.' But in 1826, the critic William Hazlitt suggested in his essay 'Whether genius is conscious of its powers?': 'No really great man ever thought himself so…He who comes up to his own idea of greatness, must always have had a very low standard of it in his mind.' Picasso, for instance, said publicly: 'When I am alone with myself, I cannot regard myself as an artist. In the strict sense of the word. The great painters were Giotto, Rembrandt, and Goya.'

The scientific study of genius began with the publication in 1869 of *Hereditary Genius: An Inquiry into Its Laws and Consequences* by Darwin's cousin Francis Galton, the founder of psychology, who conducted detailed research on the backgrounds, lives, and achievements of illustrious individuals and their relatives, deceased and living. But strangely, there is hardly a mention of 'genius' in Galton's book; no attempt is made to define genius; and no entry for 'genius' appears in the book's index (unlike

1. *The Apotheosis of Homer*, painting by Jean August Dominique Ingres, 1827

'intelligence'). When Galton published a second edition in 1892, he regretted his title and wished he could change it to *Hereditary Ability*. 'There was not the slightest intention on my part to use the word genius in any technical sense, but merely as expressing an ability that was exceptionally high,' he wrote in a new preface. 'There is much that is indefinite in the application of the word genius. It is applied to many a youth by his contemporaries, but more rarely by biographers, who do not always agree among themselves.'

That unavoidable imprecision persists, despite a somewhat improved understanding of the ingredients of genius and its patterns during the 20th century. 'I have always been wary of attempts to generalize about genius...There seems to be no common denominator except uncommonness', writes the historian Roy Porter in his foreword to *Genius and the Mind*, a collection of academic 'studies of creativity and temperament',

**2. Pablo Picasso, 1904. How do we decide which individuals are geniuses, and which are not?**

edited by the psychologist Andrew Steptoe, published in 1998. 'And yet,... as a historian I cannot help being fascinated by genius.' The imprecision is reflected in the varying stature of those discussed in this book, of whom a mere handful are undisputed geniuses like Mozart and Einstein. There cannot be a consensus on exactly who is, and is not, a genius. Although certain individuals may be widely accepted as geniuses, the word itself resists precise definition. Indeed, this paradox is part of genius's allure – to academics studying genius almost as much as to Dr Johnson's 'every man'.

The 21st century is perhaps more fascinated by genius even than Galton's Victorian age, when geniuses like the poet Tennyson 'were in full flower', recalled Virginia Woolf, with 'long hair, great black hats, capes, and cloaks'. Geniuses in the arts and sciences – the focus of this book – such as Leonardo and Newton, grip the imagination of generation after generation. So does the military and political genius of Napoleon, Churchill, and Gandhi, and the 'evil genius' of Hitler, Stalin, and Mao. Genius is also a word lavishly applied to top performers in activities as varied as chess, sports, and music. Moreover, the accolade may not only be bestowed but also withdrawn by experts and the public, as the prize-winning and sensationally successful British installation artist Damien Hirst discovered. In response to devastating reviews of his inaugural exhibition of paintings in 2009, Hirst vowed to continue painting and improve. 'I don't believe in genius. I believe in freedom. I think anyone can do it. Anyone can be like Rembrandt', Hirst claimed. 'With practice, you can make great paintings.'

Galton, who coined the phrase 'nature versus nurture', would certainly have disagreed. He was an exceptionally intelligent member of the Darwin family; his maternal grandfather, Erasmus Darwin, was the paternal grandfather of Charles Darwin. It was the publication of his first cousin's book about natural selection, *On the Origin of Species*, in 1859, which persuaded Galton that high intelligence and genius must be inherited. By ranking the abilities of past and present 'men of eminence' – mainly but not exclusively Englishmen – and searching for the occurrence of eminence in families, Galton hoped to prove his thesis, as set out in the opening words of his introductory chapter:

> I propose to show in this book that a man's natural abilities are
> derived by inheritance, under exactly the same limitations as are
> the form and physical features of the whole organic world.

To obtain his data on eminence, Galton made the reasonable but
problematic assumption that high reputation is an accurate
indicator of high ability. He then analysed the records of
achievements and honours set out in three printed sources: a
leading contemporary biographical handbook, *Men of the Time*;
the obituary of the year 1868 published in *The Times* newspaper;
and obituaries published in England going back into the past. If
he were working today, he would no doubt have analysed lists of
Nobel prize-winners, too. On this basis, Galton arbitrarily defined
an 'eminent' person as someone who had achieved a position
attained by only 250 persons in each million, that is one person in
every 4,000. (He argued for this number poetically, since 4,000 is
perhaps the number of stars visible to the naked eye on the most
brilliant of starlit nights – 'yet we feel it to be an extraordinary
distinction to a star to be accounted as the brightest in the sky'.)
An 'illustrious' person – much rarer than an eminent one – was
one in a million, even one in many millions. 'They are men whom
the whole intelligent part of the nation mourns when they die;
who have, or deserve to have, a public funeral; and who rank in
future ages as historical characters.' As already noted, Galton left a
'genius' undefined.

The bulk of *Hereditary Genius* consists of Galton's attempt to fit
his identified 'illustrious' and 'eminent' persons into families.
Beginning with a chapter on 'The Judges of England between
1660 and 1865', he moves through chapters on, for example,
'Literary Men', 'Men of Science', 'Musicians', 'Divines', and 'Senior
Classics of Cambridge', and concludes with 'Oarsmen' and
'Wrestlers of the North Country'. Clearly, for Galton (as for all
subsequent researchers), the idea of genius was meaningful only
when applied to a domain, such as a genius for music or a genius
for rowing.

In comparing his results obtained for different domains, Galton claimed that they supported, but did not prove, his hereditarian thesis. 'The general result is, that exactly one-half of the illustrious men have one or more eminent relations.' The highest proportion of the illustrious with an eminent family, 0.8, he found among senior judges (24 out of 30 lord chancellors) and men of science (65 out of 83), the lowest, 0.2–0.3, among divines (33 out of 196) and musicians (26 out of 100), with an overall average for all domains of 0.5. However, Galton admitted that his personal bias could easily have influenced his choice of illustrious and eminent individuals. Among the men of science, he was undoubtedly sufficiently disturbed by Newton's patent lack of intellectual ancestry or descendants to add a lengthy and unconvincing note that attempted to find signs of eminence in Newton's family. Most surprisingly, Galton failed to mention in the book some highly reputed English scientists, including the mathematician George Boole, the chemist John Dalton, the physicist Michael Faraday, the astronomer Edmond Halley, the naturalist John Ray, and the architect Christopher Wren. Faraday, the most celebrated scientist of the Victorian era, was a particularly revealing omission, since, as the son of a humble blacksmith, Faraday and his family could lend no weight to the book's thesis.

Despite Galton's finding of high inherited ability in scientists, a standard biographical study of great mathematicians, *Men of Mathematics* by the mathematician Eric Temple Bell, first published in 1937, shows just how little inherited mathematical ability is, at the highest level of achievement. Some great mathematicians came from lowly backgrounds. Newton was the son of a yeoman farmer; Carl Friedrich Gauss, the son of a gardener; Pierre-Simon Laplace, the son of a parish official and cider merchant. Others came from professional backgrounds. But of the 28 mathematicians of all time described by Bell, beginning with Zeno in the 5th century BC, where ancestral information is available, it shows that there is hardly a trace of mathematical achievement to be found in any of the fathers and close relatives.

Intriguing though Galton's eminent families are, they decidedly do not demonstrate the inheritance of genius. For there is a basic flaw in his analysis: his criteria for genius (which, of course, Galton never defines) are not strict enough, allowing in too many high achievers whose distinction may be considerable but is far from enduringly exceptional. *Hereditary Genius* is, so to speak, closer to the Queen's honours list than the Nobel prize. (Whether or not the Nobel prize is good at distinguishing genius, we shall come to in Chapter 10.) When Galton speaks of the heritability of 'a man's natural abilities' in his thesis, what he really seems to mean is the heritability of talent, rather than genius. As most psychologists now agree, the evidence for some inheritance of talent is considerable, though nowhere near as convincing as Galton claimed, whilst the evidence for inherited genius is slight or non-existent.

Distinguishing talent from genius is inevitably fraught with difficulty, since neither term has a widely agreed definition or method of measurement. The most obvious question to ask is whether talent and genius form a continuum, or are separated by a discontinuity? Put another way, the question becomes: should we speak of greater and lesser geniuses – instead of simply genius? Physicists generally feel that Einstein is a greater genius than, say, his contemporary Niels Bohr (also a Nobel laureate). Artists feel the same about Picasso, as compared with his contemporary Georges Braque. And the same is true for composers regarding Mozart, as compared with his contemporary (and fervent admirer) Joseph Haydn.

Rankings of composers throw some light on this issue. During the 20th century, various rankings were compiled by psychologists, based on asking orchestral players and musicologists to rate lists of composers in order of significance, and also on tabulating the frequency of performance of a composer's work. In 1933, the members of four leading American orchestras were given a list of 17 names of the best-known classical composers, plus the names

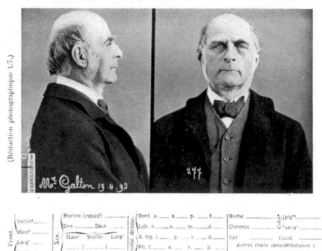

3. **Francis Galton, founder of scientific research into genius, posed as a criminal on a visit to the pioneering Criminal Identification Laboratory in Paris, 1893**

of two modern popular composers, so as to create a reference point. All four orchestras ranked Beethoven top, at number 1, and the two modern popular composers (Edward MacDowell and Victor Herbert) bottom, at numbers 18 and 19. They also all ranked J. S. Bach, Johannes Brahms, Mozart, Richard Wagner, and Franz Schubert high, and ranked Edvard Grieg, César Franck, Giuseppe Verdi, and Igor Stravinsky low. On average, Brahms was at number 2, Mozart at 3, Wagner at 4, Bach at 5, and Schubert at 6. (Amazingly, George Frederick Handel was not one of the 19 composers on the list.) A similar survey, but this time of 100 composers, answered by members of the American Musicological

Society in 1969, produced similar rankings to the 1933 survey, though now with Bach at number 1, Beethoven at 2, and Mozart still at 3 (and Handel now at 6). Around the same time, 1968, a third survey – this time of performance frequencies – showed Mozart as the most performed composer, followed by Beethoven, then Bach, Wagner, Brahms, and Schubert, in that order. So there are some grounds for thinking that 'Taste is lawful', in the words of the 1969 survey.

But what is perhaps more interesting is the fuller result of the 1933 survey. When each musician was asked to compare each of the 19 composers with each of the rest and indicate his preference, and their rankings were then suitably scaled and plotted on a graph of falling preference against increasing rank number 1–19, the line of the graph was seen to fall gradually from Beethoven to Grieg (before dropping precipitately down to MacDowell and Herbert). The drop in performance frequencies of the 100 composers in the 1968 survey was also gradual, from Mozart at number 1 to Giuseppe Tartini at number 100, without any obvious breaks. An abrupt drop in performance frequency would seem to indicate a discontinuity between genius and talent – but such a drop was not observed.

If talent is a necessary component of genius – necessary, co-extensive, but not sufficient – of what does talent consist? Inherited ability? Passion? Determination? Capacity for hard practice? Responsiveness to coaching? A combination of all of these?

The relationship between inherited ability and long practice is the most contentious aspect of talent. It is very difficult to disentangle genetic from environmental influences. There are seven parent–child pairs of Nobel laureates in science, for example. But it is impossible to determine how much of the success of the child was genetically determined. In addition to having shared genes, William and Lawrence Bragg literally worked together (hence their joint Nobel prize); Aage Bohr worked for decades at his father Niels Bohr's Institute of Theoretical Physics; while Irène Joliot-Curie was intensively trained by her mother Marie Curie in her laboratory from early on. The fact that there are no parent–child pairs among Nobel laureates in literature (admittedly a much smaller number of individuals than in science), where training is largely solitary, is at least suggestive that training may be more important to success than inherited talent.

Mozart, famously, is a compelling instance of the difficulty. He was the son of a considerable musician: the violinist, music teacher, and composer Leopold Mozart. He also had musical relatives on his mother's side of the family. So he surely inherited some musical ability. But at the same time, he underwent a unique course of training at the hands of his father, a hard driver and an inspired teacher, who controlled Wolfgang's life for over two decades. However, there is a way of separating the effect of the Mozart family genes from the family training which is not normally available. Wolfgang's elder sister Maria Anna, known as Nannerl – four and a half years older than him – who naturally shared half of his genes, was also a talented piano player as a child. She too was exposed to the intensive training of Leopold, side by side with her brother. As soon as the children were ready, Leopold took them on a tour of the courts and major cities of Europe in 1763–6, where together they became celebrities. Yet, Nannerl did not go on to compose, unlike her brother. Why not?

The obvious explanation will not do. Women in the 18th century were permitted to excel in music, if not in many other fields; and several did. And there is no plausible reason why the hugely ambitious Leopold would have chosen to hold Nannerl back during her teenage years in the 1760s, long before the premature death of her mother (after which Nannerl had to act as a companion to her demanding father). 'I suggest the explanation for Nannerl Mozart's lack of progression beyond performance is that she lacked the capacity for creating original music', writes the psychologist Andrew Steptoe, who has written a major study of Mozart's operas.

> There is a strong case for supposing that the differences between the capacities of the two people who emerged were the product of their personal biological endowments. On the other hand, it is indisputable that without the intense nurturance provided by Leopold, Wolfgang's creativity would not have blossomed.

Mozart's musical ability was transparently obvious to his father (and sister) in childhood, as has been the case with many successful musicians and some composers. This fact has lent credence to the common view – predominant among music educators – that talent is essentially innate: you are born with it and cannot acquire it, though you can (and must) hone it, if you want to make a profession out of it. Thus, people often say that someone they know plays an instrument well because she has innate talent. How do they know she has talent? It's obvious – because she plays so well!

Nonetheless, hundreds of studies by psychologists, conducted over decades, have failed to provide unimpeachable evidence for the existence of innate talent. Although there is certainly evidence of a genetic contribution to intelligence (see Chapter 4), the correlations between general intelligence and various specific abilities – such as playing a musical instrument well – are small. No genes 'for' domain-specific talents have yet been located, although the search continues. Furthermore, the indisputable and astonishing improvement in performance standards observed during the past century, in sports, chess, music, and some other fields, has happened much too fast to be explained by genetic changes, which would require thousands of years. Rather than genes operating alone, psychologists' study of talent suggests the importance of the other factors mentioned above: passion, determination, practice, and coaching.

In one study, young students at a music school were divided into two groups based on the evaluation of their ability by teachers – that is, the teachers' perception of the students' talent. The division was done secretly, so as not to bias the students' future performance. After several years, the highest performance ratings were achieved by those students who had practised the most in the intervening period, irrespective of which 'talent' group their teachers had earlier allotted them to. In another study, by the music psychologist Gary McPherson, children were asked a simple question before they started their first music lesson: 'How long do you think you will play your new instrument?' The options were: through this year, through primary school, through high school, or throughout life. On the basis of their answers, McPherson categorized the children (again in secret) into three groups, showing short-term commitment, medium-term commitment, and long-term commitment. He then measured the amount of practice by each child per week and came up with three more categories: low (20 minutes per week), medium (45 minutes per week), and high (90 minutes per week). When he plotted the children's actual performance on a graph, the differences between the three groups were astonishing. Not only did the long-term committed perform better with a low level of practice than the short-term committed with a high level of practice (presumably forced by their parents!) – the long-term committed performed 400 per cent better than the short-term committed when they, too, adopted a high level of practice.

Recent neuroscientific research offers clear evidence for the physiological effects of determined practice. The brain is plastic, and it alters through practice. One of the best-known studies, published in 2000 by Eleanor Maguire and colleagues, used functional magnetic resonance imaging (fMRI) to examine the hippocampus of London taxi-drivers. Practising their spatial memory assiduously had measurably increased the size of the drivers' hippocampi relative to the hippocampi of a control group. Moreover, the increase in size correlated with the number of years the driver had spent on the job.

Other studies have looked at musicians. One published in 2005 used another MRI technique known as diffusion tensor imaging (DTI), sensitive to changes in white rather than grey matter, to investigate the brains of professional pianists. Its main author, Fredrik Ullén, is a piano virtuoso as well as a neuroscientist, interested in the effect of musical practice on white matter. Myelin, the white fatty substance that sheaths the conducting axons (thread-like nerve fibres) of the adult brain, like plastic insulation around a wire, was found by Ullén to grow gradually thicker with practice, increasing the strength of the DTI signal. The more a pianist practised over time, the thicker was the myelin, the less leaky and more efficient the axons, and the better the communication system of the brain's synapses and neurons.

Certainly white matter is key to types of learning that require prolonged practice and repetition, as well as extensive integration among greatly separated regions of the cerebral cortex. Children whose brains are still myelinating widely find it much easier to acquire new skills than their grandparents do,

thinks the neuroscientist R. Douglas Fields.

So practice can, it seems, do much to perfect the brain for specific tasks, such as playing the piano, chess, or tennis. But of course the brain initially forms and develops under the direction of an individual's genome, like every other part of the body, uninfluenced by conscious decisions. Which brings us back to the knotty problem of the genetic or innate element in talent.

Since this has, as yet, no solution, the best that can be offered is probably the analysis of two psychologists and a musicologist, Michael Howe, John Sloboda, and Jane Davidson, who together surveyed the entire scientific literature on talent. In 1998, they came to the following cautious conclusions: 'individual differences in some special abilities may indeed have partly genetic origins'; and that 'there do exist some attributes that are possessed by only a minority of individuals. In this very restricted sense, talent may be said to exist.' Overall, however, they claimed that 'there may be little or no basis for innate giftedness', and that the prevalence of the idea in education (especially music teaching) produces the undesirable effect of discriminating against able children who might otherwise become 'talented' adults. Some psychologists agree with them, but others strongly disagree.

Genius is even more problematic than talent – its definition and measurement still embroiled in the arguments that dogged Galton's *Hereditary Genius*. It would be absurd to deny the existence of genius, faced by the achievements of, say, Leonardo and Newton. But it would be equally absurd to insist that genius has nothing at all to do with 'mere talent', as witness John Bardeen, a double Nobel laureate in physics (the only one) who worked constantly at physics but was not regarded as a genius either by himself or other physicists. Although genius is never inherited or passed on, it seems, like talent, to be partly genetic in origin in many cases, as with Leopold and Wolfgang Mozart, or Erasmus and Charles Darwin. Unlike talent, though, genius is the result of a unique configuration of parental genes and personal circumstances. Since a genius never transmits the full complement of his or her genes – only a half-helping – to offspring, whose personal circumstances inevitably differ from those of the parent genius, this configuration never repeats itself in the offspring. Thus, it is not surprising that genius does not run in families, but that talent sometimes does.

# Chapter 2
## Family affairs

In all cultures, there are famously talented families: the Bach family in Germany, the Bernoullis in Switzerland, the Darwins and the Huxleys in Britain, the Tagores in India, the Tolstoys in Russia, for instance. Yet, even among the several distinguished individuals bearing the names Bach, Bernoulli, Darwin, Tagore, or Tolstoy, there is only one generally accepted genius: Johann Sebastian Bach, Daniel Bernoulli, Charles Darwin, Rabindranath Tagore, and Leo Tolstoy.

That genius does not run in families was illustrated by the artist Giorgio Vasari in his 16th-century *Lives* of the leading Renaissance artists: most came from non-creative origins, including Leonardo da Vinci, Michelangelo, and Titian (scions of minor legal, banking, and official families, respectively). Galton proved it, if unintentionally, in his *Hereditary Genius*, by demonstrating that talent, rather than genius, seems to be partially hereditary (especially among English judges). Great names like Shakespeare, Bernini, Newton, Beethoven, Faraday, Byron, Gauss, Cézanne, and Einstein occur but once in the roll-call of genius. A genius has yet to beget another genius.

By contrast, a distinguished creative family may periodically beget a genius. The Darwin family provides one well-known example.

Charles Darwin was the grandson of two eminent figures: the physician, biologist, and writer Erasmus Darwin, and the potter Josiah Wedgwood. Another is the family of Virginia Woolf, who came from a line of scholars and writers on her paternal side, the Stephens, most notably her father Leslie Stephen, founder editor of *The Dictionary of National Biography*, and on her mother's side the photographer Julia Margaret Cameron. Less well known is that Tagore was the son of a leading Bengali religious figure, Debendranath Tagore, and the grandson of India's first industrial entrepreneur, Dwarkanath Tagore.

A correlation between heredity and exceptional creativity is therefore problematic, although clearly some relationship between them does exist. What about an environmental influence, a role for parental nurture – and also parental rejection? Here, too, we might expect to find some connection with genius.

One of the most interesting patterns among geniuses concerns the effect of the early loss of a parent. A survey of 699 famous historical personages conducted by the psychologist J. M. Eisenstadt in 1978 revealed that 25 per cent of them had lost at least one parent before the age of 10, 34.5 per cent before the age of 15, 45 per cent before the age of 20, and 52 per cent – more than half – before the age of 26. Instances include J. S. Bach, Robert Boyle, Samuel Taylor Coleridge, Dante, Darwin, Antoine Lavoisier, Michelangelo, Newton, Peter Paul Rubens, Tolstoy, Richard Wagner, and Orson Welles, all of whom lost one or both parents in their first decade of life; and Hans Christian Andersen, Beethoven, Marie Curie, Humphry Davy, Edgar Degas, Fyodor Dostoevsky, George Frederick Handel, Robert Hooke, Victor Hugo, August Kekulé, Tagore, Mark Twain, and Virginia Woolf, all of whom lost one or both parents in their second decade. Certainly, these mortality figures tell us nothing definite about orphanhood and genius without access to the mortality figures for the general population during the same period; and such estimates of life expectancy are tricky to make until we reach quite recent times.

But they are supported by figures from the early 20th century, such as a survey of eminent American scientists by Anne Roe in 1953, which tend to show that the death of a mother or both parents by the age of 15 is around three times more frequent (26 per cent) among the eminent than among the general population (8 per cent). That is about the same relative frequency of early parental mortality as for those who become delinquents or suicidal depressives, compared to the general population.

This naturally raises the issue of why some children become stronger through the loss of a parent, while others are weakened and even destroyed. In the words of Winston Churchill (whose father Randolph died tragically in 1895, when his son was 21):

> Solitary trees, if they grow at all grow strong; and a boy deprived of a father's care often develops, if he escapes the perils of youth, an independence and vigour of thought which may restore in after life the heavy loss of early days.

Virginia Woolf suffered her first nervous breakdown as a result of her mother's early death in 1895, followed by a period of excruciating tension with her widower father that eventually precipitated her next breakdown after his death in 1904. What was it in her that permitted her to recover, at least for a while, and make a career as a writer, rather than withdraw into despair and creative sterility, or worse, in her formative years?

The reasons are no doubt complicated, and differ for different individuals, according to their development and circumstances at the time of their bereavement. Darwin noted in his autobiography that as a child aged 8 he was barely aware of his mother's death, whereas Curie, at a similar age when her mother died, sank into 'a profound depression', according to her autobiography. The response to the early death of a parent must inevitably involve a mixture of conflicting emotions and motives, ranging from anxiety to anger, from an urge for self-preservation and security to a desire for self-advertisement and love. But why should creativity – and even genius – sometimes emerge from this experience of youthful trauma?

Various explanations have been proposed by psychologists. One suggestion is that creative achievement, delinquency, and suicide should all be viewed as dissatisfied responses to the society that took away the life of the parent. By criticizing or attacking existing social beliefs and practices, creative achievement enables an individual to develop in an independent, nonconformist way, rejecting society's rules and regulations. Another suggestion is that creative production offers an outlet for coping with feelings of isolation, sadness, guilt, and unworthiness arising from abandonment by the deceased parent which would otherwise prove self-destructive. A third possibility is that the admiration, prestige, and power that can derive from creative achievement may allow achievers to manipulate and dominate those around them, so that they feel in control of their destiny and can protect themselves from receiving further shocks.

The psychiatrist and psychoanalyst Karen Horney proposed that the possible reactions to early bereavement have three basic goals. In 'turning towards people', the individual solicits their love, approval, admiration, and protection – quite like the affable young Darwin; in 'turning away from people', he or she withdraws and seeks independence and self-sufficiency, perfection, and unassailability – rather like the 'impudent' young Einstein (his own adjective); lastly, in 'turning against people', he or she seeks power, prestige, and domination, or exploits them – definitely like the irascible Newton and perhaps also Leonardo. Creative achievement is capable of bringing all these goals within reach of individuals. As the psychologist Mihaly Csikszentmihalyi sums up, in his study of creativity based on interviews in the 1990s with nearly 100 creative individuals (12 of them Nobel laureates):

> While creative adults often overcome the blow of being orphaned, Jean-Paul Sartre's aphorism that the greatest gift a father can give

his son is to die early is an exaggeration. There are just too many examples of a warm and stimulating family context to conclude that hardship or conflict is necessary to unleash the creative urge. In fact, creative individuals seem to have had either exceptionally supportive childhoods or very deprived and challenging ones. What appears to be missing is the vast middle ground.

Nevertheless, other surveys suggest a preponderance of deprived over supportive childhoods among the highly creative. A study of 400 eminent historical figures, *Cradles of Eminence*, published in 1962 by the psychologists Victor and Mildred Goertzel, found that 75 per cent of the eminent had suffered broken homes and rejection by their parents. More than one in four had a physical handicap. A later study of 300 eminent figures from the 20th century, also by the Goertzels, found an even higher incidence, 85 per cent, of very troubled home backgrounds – highest (89 per cent) among novelists and playwrights, lowest (56 per cent) among scientists. It is also the case that literary Nobel laureates come more often from poor backgrounds than scientific laureates, and suffer more physical disabilities than them. 'From the evidence, one may indeed go so far as to suggest that creators typically suffered some deprivation and distress in childhood', writes R. Ochse in his excellent study of the determinants of genius.

Some were bereaved of parents, some were rejected, some were sternly disciplined. Some were exposed to emotional tensions, financial insecurities, or physical hardships. Some were overprotected, lonely, or insecure, and some were ugly, deformed, or physically disabled. Many suffered several of these hardships in combination.

Anecdotal evidence from novelists tends to confirm this picture, even after making due allowance for the embellishment of childhood memories by a sensitive adult writer. Charles Dickens's childhood miseries were legion. Joseph Conrad recalled his childhood between the ages of 8 and 12 – that is, between the deaths of his mother and his father from tuberculosis – as follows:

> I don't know what would have become of me if I had not been a reading boy. My prep finished, I would have nothing to do but sit and watch the awful stillness of the sickroom flow through the closed door and coldly enfold my scared heart. I suppose that in a futile childish way I would have gone crazy. Often, not always, I cried myself into a good sound sleep.

Anton Chekhov, who was the son of a struggling grocer who had been born a serf, had painful, though creatively productive, memories of childhood. 'Despotism and lies so disfigured our childhood that it makes me sick and horrified to think of it', he wrote.

> I remember father began to teach me, or to put it more plainly, whip me, when I was only five years old. He whipped me, boxed my ears, hit me over the head, and the first question I asked myself on awakening every morning was 'Will I be whipped today?' I was forbidden to play games or romp.

The idea that genius is fostered by such extreme childhood circumstances – whether of adversity and conflict or support and love – is a tempting one. It is easy to believe that exceptional creativity must be the product of exceptional emotions. However, the home environments of geniuses only partially confirm the validity of this simple picture, whilst at the same time complicating it.

At one extreme, Leonardo unquestionably suffered from extreme parental neglect, since he was abandoned by his father and mother in infancy, except for his father's seminal introduction of the teenaged Leonardo to the artist Andrea del Verrocchio and his studio. At the other extreme, Mozart was cosseted by his father, mother, and sister, during his every waking minute from infancy until his early twenties. Through his father's full-time tuition and promotion, Mozart's music-making was given every available encouragement to flourish. Einstein, however, occupies the middle ground, mentioned by Csikszentmihalyi, so far as his immediate family were concerned: neither much neglected nor much encouraged. At no point did Einstein's parents or close relatives discourage his teenaged interest in mathematics and theoretical physics, but neither did they greet it with enthusiasm (there are no letters to his engineer-businessman father about physics, for example) – that was left to friends, entirely outside the Einstein family circle.

Rather than allotting geniuses either a 'supportive' or a 'deprived' childhood, it is truer to say their creativity seems to emerge from a tension or conflict between support and deprivation. To

4. Portrait of the Mozart family by Johann Nepomuk della Croce, 1780–1. From left to right: Maria Anna (Nannerl), Wolfgang Amadeus, and Leopold Mozart; the oval portrait shows Mozart's deceased mother, Anna Maria

oversimplify, the young Leonardo certainly lacked parental love and direction, but as a consequence he enjoyed unusual freedom to explore alone, both literally in Vinci and Florence, and also figuratively in art and science. Mozart's fanatical supervision by his father undoubtedly hampered his development as an autonomous individual, but allowed him to blossom as a musician and performer; only when he broke with his father in his mid-twenties could he realize himself fully as a composer. Einstein's lack of involvement with his parents, and his rebellion against their choice of school and their conventional social values, surely helped to prepare the ground and give him the confidence to effect his revolutionary transformation of physics, which overturned the conventional understanding of light, space, and time.

Support is a social act, which raises a further aspect of the relationship between family, friends, and genius: the question of sociability versus solitude in exceptional creativity. The historian Edward Gibbon wrote in his memoirs that: 'conversation enriches the mind, but solitude is the school of genius' – and it is clear that most geniuses have agreed with this. However useful others may have been in stimulating their minds, their best ideas came to them when alone. The statue of Newton in the chapel of Trinity College Cambridge is, according to William Wordsworth's *Prelude*, 'the marble index of a mind forever Voyaging through strange seas of Thought, alone'. Thomas Alva Edison, although acutely conscious of the importance of societal demand and marketability in inventing, said: 'the best thinking has been done in solitude'. Pierre Curie wrote in his youthful diary (as reported by Marie Curie):

> Whenever, rotating slowly upon myself, I attempt to speed up,
> the merest nothing – a word, a story, a newspaper, a visit – stops
> me, prevents my becoming a gyroscope or top, and can postpone
> or forever delay the instant when, equipped with sufficient speed,
> I might be able to concentrate within myself in spite of what is
> around me.

Wagner noted that: 'isolation and complete loneliness are my only consolation and my salvation'. Byron stated: 'society is harmful to any achievement of the mind'; and his friend Samuel Taylor Coleridge blamed the interruption of 'a person on business from Porlock' for stymieing the dream-induced composition of his poem 'Kubla Khan'. V. S. Naipaul believed: 'Writing comes from the most secret recesses of the person, and the writer himself does not know those recesses. So it's a kind of magic.'

So much for solitary geniuses in adulthood. Are they solitary in childhood, too? According to Ochse's study, they tend to be. 'Another recurrent theme in the literature on the childhood of creative achievers is social isolation and loneliness', he writes.

> Many creative achievers were isolated from other children because of restrictions placed upon them by parents; illness; constant movement of the family from one community to another; lack of siblings; or natural shyness. For whatever reason, it seems that creators typically engaged in solitary activities in childhood.

Conrad, for example, was an only child, forced to leave his native Poland at the age of 4 with his mother when his patriot father was exiled to the harsh climate of northern Russia, and then was orphaned by the deaths of both parents. Even Mozart, for all his childhood love of public performing, could be solitary as a child. In one telling incident on tour in 1765 when he was 9, Mozart's bedridden sister Nannerl lay close to death from a fever, watched over by her anxious parents, while 'little Wolfgang in the next room was amusing himself with his music', as noted by Leopold Mozart.

Thus, collaboration and teamwork tend not to be a feature of the lives of the exceptionally creative – inconvenient though this fact may be for advocates of 'brainstorming' and 'group creativity' in commercial companies and other institutions. Genius does not sit well on committees. It perhaps goes without saying that the greatest poetry, novels, paintings, music, and even films, are almost always the vision of one person – hence the fact that the Nobel prize for literature has almost always been awarded to a single individual. Plainly this is not true of science and scientific Nobel prizes. Science is by its very nature collaborative, particularly in recent decades; and there have been some celebrated scientific partnerships, such as Marie Curie with her husband Pierre Curie, William Bragg with his son Lawrence Bragg (X-ray crystallography), Francis Crick with James Watson (the molecular structure of DNA), and Michael Ventris with John Chadwick (the decipherment of the Minoan script Linear B). Yet, it is still the case that the most revered scientists – Galileo, Newton, Faraday, Darwin, Einstein, and some others – have published their most important work alone.

The roles of partners and offspring provide the final pattern in considering family and genius. Whatever their real talents and contributions may have been, the wives, husbands, and children of geniuses have typically seemed insubstantial or totally forgotten figures in the eyes of posterity. In encyclopaedias and reference books, they are often relegated to a mere sentence or phrase, if that, even in the case of Darwin, whose loyal wife Emma Wedgwood, 'the patient ghost behind his never-ending struggle for perfection' (biographer Janet Browne's words), acted as a significant and necessary editor of her husband Charles's often tangled prose, including *On the Origin of Species*, and discussed many of his ideas with him; and whose sons in some cases distinguished themselves in science. Perhaps this is inevitable, especially when wives, husbands, and children try to achieve in the same domain as their eminent partner or parent, as Einstein's first wife, Mileva Marić, attempted to do in physics and Mozart's second son, also called Wolfgang Amadeus, attempted to do in musical performance. (Einstein's first son, Hans Albert, deliberately avoided theoretical physics, and became a hydraulic engineer.) Such partners and children will always be compared and found wanting.

Even here, though, there are major exceptions. Both Marie Curie and Virginia Woolf married distinguished creative figures, who became stimulating partners of genius. Collaboration with Pierre Curie brought out the best in Marie – a fact openly recognized by both her and by the Swedish Academy in its award of the Nobel prize for physics for their joint discovery of radium; in addition, the Curies' eldest daughter later shared the Nobel prize for chemistry with her husband. The writer and journalist Leonard Woolf was, if anything, even more crucial to Virginia Woolf. A sensitive and honest critic and editor of her work (judging from her comments on him in her famous diary), Leonard saved her from suicide when she was writing her first novel in 1913, a year after their marriage. In her much-quoted last letter, before she drowned herself in the river in 1941, Virginia told Leonard:

> What I want to say is that I owe all the happiness of my life to you. You have been entirely patient with me and incredibly good. I want to say that – everybody knows it. If anybody could have saved me it would have been you. Everything has gone from me but the certainty of your goodness. I cant go on spoiling your life any longer. I dont think two people could have been happier than we have been. V.

Thus, the influence of family upbringing and environment on the development of genius operates in many ways, both positive and negative, as we might expect. Genius has flourished in the near-absence of parents as well as in their loving presence. But other than geniuses' predilection for solitude at all ages, the influence is not susceptible to generalization.

# Chapter 3
# The schooling of genius

Compared with the family, formal education has a less complex, generally uneasy, relationship with genius. Consider the astonishing life of the early 20th-century Indian mathematician Srinivasa Ramanujan, whom current mathematicians regard as one of the great mathematicians of all time, in a class with Leonhard Euler and Karl Jacobi according to Bell's *Men of Mathematics*.

In barest outline, Ramanujan, born in 1887 to poor parents, was an impoverished, devoutly Brahmin clerk working at the Madras Port Trust, self-taught in mathematics and without a university degree, who claimed that his mathematics was inspired by a Hindu goddess, Namagiri. He used to say: 'An equation for me has no meaning, unless it represents a thought of God.' Out of desperation at the dearth of appreciation of his theorems by university-trained mathematicians in India, in 1913 Ramanujan mailed some of the theorems, without proofs, to a leading Cambridge University mathematician (and confirmed atheist), G. H. Hardy. Despite their unfamiliar and highly improbable source, so transcendently original were the formulae that Hardy dragged a reluctant Ramanujan from obscurity to Trinity College Cambridge, collaborated extensively with him, published many joint papers in journals, and demonstrated that he was a mathematical genius. In 1918, Ramanujan was elected the first

Indian fellow of Trinity College and of the modern Royal Society. But, having fallen mysteriously ill, and having attempted suicide on the London Underground, he returned to India to recuperate, still producing major new theorems on his sickbed, and died tragically at the age of just 32.

After his death, a dazzled Hardy wrote of Ramanujan:

> The limitations of his knowledge were as startling as its profundity...His ideas as to what constituted a mathematical proof were of the most shadowy description. All his results, new and old, right or wrong, had been arrived at by a process of mingled argument, intuition, and induction, of which he was entirely unable to give any coherent account.

Ramanujan's biographer Robert Kanigel, in his masterly book *The Man Who Knew Infinity*, writes that 'Ramanujan's life was like the Bible, or Shakespeare – a rich find of data, lush with ambiguity, that holds up a mirror to ourselves or our age'. Kanigel gives four fascinating examples. First, the Indian school system flunked Ramanujan in his teens – but a few individuals in India sensed his brilliance and rescued him from near-starvation by getting him a job as a clerk. Secondly, Hardy recognized his genius from his 1913 letter – but drove him so hard in England that he may have hastened Ramanujan's death. Thirdly, had Ramanujan received Cambridge-style mathematical training in his early life, he might have reached still greater heights – but possibly, instead, such training might have stifled his originality. Lastly, Hardy, as an atheist, was convinced that religion had nothing to do with Ramanujan's intellectual power – but it is at least plausible that Hindu India's long-standing mystical attraction to the concept of the infinite was a vital source of Ramanujan's creativity. 'Was Ramanujan's life a tragedy of unfulfilled promise? Or did his five years in Cambridge redeem it?' asks Kanigel. 'In each case, the evidence [leaves] ample room to see it either way.'

**5. Srinivasa Ramanujan, 1919, mathematician of genius, before his return to India and premature death**

Ramanujan's experience of formal education can hardly be called typical. But neither should it be dismissed as unique and irrelevant. Elements of it are to be found in the education of all geniuses. While some geniuses may have enjoyed and benefited from their school days, the majority did not. (A handful never attended a school, such as Mozart and the philosopher John Stuart Mill, who were instead rigorously educated at home.) Many never went to university, or failed to distinguish themselves at university. Only a small minority became highly educated by taking a doctoral degree. Some important creative breakthroughs have emerged from colleges and universities, notably in the sciences, but on the whole they have not. Mark Twain's quip remains pertinent: 'I have never let my schooling interfere with my education.' So does that of the photographer Henri Cartier-Bresson, who failed his school leaving exam, in refusing an honorary doctorate decades later: 'What do you think I'm a professor of? The little finger?' More prosaically, the 19th-century polymath Thomas Young – physicist, physician, and Egyptologist, amongst several other things – stated, after studying at three famous universities: 'Masters and mistresses are very necessary to compensate for want of inclination and exertion: but whoever would arrive at excellence must be self-taught.' Darwin, Einstein, and many other geniuses emphatically agreed.

In 2000–2, the BBC broadcaster and arts administrator John Tusa interviewed on radio about a dozen figures in the arts concerning their creative process, and later published the conversations in full in his collection *On Creativity*. Though not geniuses, every interviewee was a leader in his or her field. They were: the architect Nicholas Grimshaw; the artists Frank Auerbach, Anthony Caro, Howard Hodgkin, and Paula Rego; the photographer Eve Arnold and the film-maker Milos Forman; the composers Harrison Birtwistle, Elliott Carter, and Gyorgy Ligeti; the writers Tony Harrison and Muriel Spark; and the art critic and curator David Sylvester. Their formal education varied greatly, from ordinary schooling in the case of Arnold and Sylvester to Carter's doctoral training in music and subsequent academic appointments. There was nothing in what they said of their careers to indicate that a basic education, let alone a university degree, is a requirement in order to be a creative person, Tusa concluded.

A much larger sample of the exceptionally creative – nearly 100 individuals – were interviewed by the University of Chicago psychologist Mihaly Csikszentmihalyi, as mentioned earlier. Unlike Tusa's subjects, Csikszentmihalyi's interviewees included, as well as those eminent in the arts, many scientists, mostly working in universities, some of whom were Nobel laureates. School days were rarely mentioned by any of the interviewees as a source of inspiration. In some cases, they remembered extracurricular school activities, for example the literary prizes won by the writer Robertson Davies or the mathematical prize won in a competition by the physicist John Bardeen. Some inspiring individual teachers were also recalled, though chiefly by the scientists. But overall, Csikszentmihalyi was surprised by how many of the interviewees had no memory of a special relationship with a teacher at school.

'It is quite strange how little effect school – even high school – seems to have had on the lives of creative people. Often one senses that, if anything, school threatened to extinguish the interest and curiosity that the child had discovered outside its walls', writes Csikszentmihalyi in his study *Creativity: Flow and the Psychology of Discovery and Invention*.

> How much did schools contribute to the accomplishments of Einstein, or Picasso, or T. S. Eliot? The record is rather grim, especially considering how much effort, how many resources, and how many hopes go into our formal educational system.

Leaving school and moving on to higher education and professional training, one finds the pattern of experiences less clear-cut. Some exceptionally creative achievers receive no further formal education after school, but this has become relatively unusual in recent decades, with the worldwide expansion in higher education; almost inconceivable for scientists. Among Tusa's sample of 20th-century creators (which excludes scientists), three of them – Arnold, Spark, and Sylvester – received no institutional training in their field, and indeed had no further formal education. Only three of them – Carter, Caro, and

Harrison – took university degrees; Carter alone went on to do a doctorate. Auerbach, Grimshaw, Hodgkin, and Rego went to art schools. Birtwistle and Ligeti trained at academies of music. Forman went to film school.

In the sciences, the saga of Einstein's physics doctorate is revealing about institutional training and creativity. In the summer of 1900, Einstein graduated from the Swiss Polytechnic, but was not offered an assistant's post in the physics department, because of his spotty attendance record at lectures and his critical attitude to the professors, leaving him in an uncomfortable situation of financial and professional uncertainty. During 1901, unable to interest professors at other institutions in employing an unknown, he decided that he needed a doctorate to make an academic career, and submitted a thesis to the University of Zurich. To his dismay, it was rejected. Then, in the summer of 1902, he at long last landed his first full-time job, at the Swiss Patent Office in Bern. The idea of a doctorate was put aside. In early 1903, Einstein told a close friend that he had abandoned the plan, 'as [it] doesn't help me much and the whole comedy has begun to bore me'. But in the summer of 1905, his *annus mirabilis*, after completing his theory of special relativity, he revived the doctorate plan for the same reason as before: he needed a doctoral degree to get out of the Patent Office and into a university.

Second time around, he submitted his paper on special relativity to the University of Zurich – and it too was rejected! At least this is what happened according to his sister, who was close to her brother: she wrote that relativity 'seemed a little uncanny to the decision-making professors'. There is no proof, although both Einstein's choice of this paper and the professors' sceptical reaction to it seem plausible, since special relativity was clearly important enough for a thesis but had not yet been vetted and published by the scientific establishment (and it would remain intensely controversial after publication, rejected by the Nobel physics committee of the Swedish Academy for many years). For whatever reason, in the end Einstein selected some less challenging, though still significant, work he had completed in April 1905, just before special relativity – a paper on how to determine the true size of molecules in liquids, respectably based on experimental data rather than relying on purely theoretical arguments like relativity – and resubmitted the thesis. According to him, perhaps half in jest, the Zurich professors informed him that the manuscript was too short, so Einstein added one sentence. Within days, this more orthodox paper was accepted, and by the end of July 1905, he could finally call himself 'Herr Doktor Einstein'. Only later was a small but important mistake discovered in the thesis, which Einstein duly corrected in print in 1906, and further refined in 1910, as better experimental data became available.

The point is, of course, that academia has an inherent tendency to ignore or reject highly original work that does not fit the existing paradigm. Einstein was self-evidently just as original and creative in 1905 without a PhD as with a PhD. To get one, he seems to have been encouraged to show less, rather than more, originality. Might it be that too much training and education can be a handicap for the truly creative? In 1984, the psychologist Dean Keith Simonton studied the education level of more than 300 exceptionally creative individuals born between 1450 and 1850, that is, those educated before the introduction of the recognizably modern university system – pre-Einstein, so to speak. Simonton discovered that the top creators – including Beethoven, Galileo, Leonardo da Vinci, Mozart, and Rembrandt van Rijn – had attained an educational level equivalent to approximately half way through a modern undergraduate programme. Those with more (or less) education than this had a lower level of creative accomplishment, generally speaking.

Not too much weight should be put on Simonton's discovery, given the difficulty of estimating the educational level of some highly creative historical individuals, and of comparing levels of education in different societies at different periods. However, the finding is supported by the regularity with which creative individuals lose interest in academic work during their undergraduate degree course and choose to focus instead on what fascinates them. A few – though none of them future scientists – even drop out of university to pursue their hunches, such as the computer programmer Bill Gates, who left Harvard University in the 1970s in order to establish Microsoft, and the film director Satyajit Ray, who dropped out of art school in India in the 1940s to become a commercial artist.

Simonton's finding may also provide a clue as to why, in higher education, the post-war increase in the number of PhDs has not led to more exceptionally creative research – if Simonton is correct that the optimal education for exceptional creativity does not require a PhD. In the sciences, the 20th-century expansion of higher education at doctoral level produced a proliferation of new research specialisms and new journals catering to these specialisms. 'Since 1945, the number of scientific papers and journals in highly industrialized societies – particularly in the United States – has risen almost exponentially, while the proportion of the workforce in research and development and the percentage of gross national product devoted to it have grown more modestly', the sociologist of science J. Rogers Hollingsworth wrote in *Nature* in 2008, after spending several decades studying innovation in different societies. 'Yet the rate at which truly creative work emerges has remained relatively constant. In terms of the scale of research efforts to make major scientific breakthroughs, there are diminishing returns.'

A more likely explanation of this fact, however, is that in contemporary society exceptionally creative scientists and artists differ in the periods of training they require, because of the changed nature of the scientific enterprise, as compared to that of the late 19th century and before. Exceptionally creative artists do not require doctoral training now any more than they did in earlier times – but this is not true of their equivalents in science, who must master a greater breadth of knowledge and techniques before they can reach the frontier of their discipline and make a new discovery.

Scientists also need to be much better students than artists, in terms of their performance in school and university examinations. Simonton notes that: 'the contrast in academic performance between scientists and artists appears to reflect the comparative degree of constraint that must be imposed on the creative process in the sciences versus the arts.' Whether this fact has the tendency to squeeze out of the system potential Darwins and Einsteins in favour of the merely productive academic scientist is an endlessly discussed subject, to which no one has yet given a satisfactory answer. What is generally accepted, though, is that the huge growth in size and competitiveness of higher education in the second half of the 20th century and after, did not increase the number of exceptionally creative scientists.

The decipherment of the Minoan Linear B script by Michael Ventris in 1952 – a breakthrough cutting across art and science that was dubbed the 'Everest of Greek archaeology' – illustrates well much of what we have just discussed. Like Ramanujan's mathematical theorems, Ventris's unexpected discovery that the language written in Linear B was Mycenaean Greek required both self-training and exceptional creativity, but no undergraduate degree or PhD.

Although the challenge of reading the ancient Minoan script excavated at Knossos in 1900 by Arthur Evans had attracted the attentions of dozens of scholars during the first half of the 20th century, the five key figures in the decipherment were Emmett Bennett Jr, Alice Kober, John Myres, John Chadwick, and Ventris. Bennett was an epigraphist, with wartime experience of cryptography, who had written a doctorate on Linear B under the archaeologist Carl Blegen at the University of Cincinnati in the

**6. Michael Ventris, 1952, a professional architect who in his spare time deciphered Minoan Linear B, Europe's earliest readable writing**

late 1940s; soon after this, he moved to Yale University. Kober was a classicist with a PhD in Greek literature from Columbia University, who had developed a consuming interest in Linear B in the mid-1930s. The ageing Myres was professor of ancient history at Oxford University until 1939 and was widely considered a leading authority on the ancient Greeks; in addition, he had become the custodian and editor of the Linear B tablets after the death of his friend Evans in 1941. Chadwick had an undergraduate degree in classics from Cambridge University but no PhD; after wartime service as a cryptographer and work in Oxford on the staff of the *Oxford Latin Dictionary*, he became a lecturer in classics at Cambridge in 1952, the year he began collaborating with Ventris. Unlike the other four, Ventris never went to university and had no professional training in classics, other than at school, where his passion to decipher Linear B began as a 14-year-old. Instead, Ventris underwent training as an architect at the Architectural Association School in London in the

1940s – interrupted by war service – before beginning to practise architecture professionally.

Bennett, Kober, Myres, and Chadwick were all older than Ventris; were better trained than him in classical studies; and had more opportunity than him to concentrate on the problem of 'cracking' Linear B. Yet they all failed, where he succeeded. One is compelled to ask why.

There are many reasons (which I discuss in my book about Ventris, *The Man Who Deciphered Linear B*). But the most important ones are: first, the fact that Ventris was knowledgeable in three very different domains – classics, modern languages, and architecture; and secondly, that as an architect he did not have the same investment as the professional scholars in orthodox thinking about Linear B. Myres, for instance, was hamstrung by the incorrect theories of the extremely influential Evans. Kober, though brilliantly logical, was temperamentally unwilling to hazard guesses. She wrote of Linear B in 1948: 'When we have the facts, certain conclusions will be almost inevitable. Until we have them, no conclusions are possible.' Bennett, though highly intelligent, suffered too from scholarly over-restraint: he greeted the decipherment in public with a 'fine set of cautious, non-committal phrases' (as he privately admitted to Ventris). In a sense, Ventris succeeded because he did not have a degree or a doctorate in classics. He had enough training in the subject, but not too much to curtail his curiosity and originality. As his collaborator Chadwick nicely says in his book, *The Decipherment of Linear B*:

> The architect's eye sees in a building not a mere facade, a jumble of ornamental and structural features; it looks beneath the appearance and distinguishes the significant parts of the building. So too Ventris was able to discern among the bewildering variety of the mysterious signs, patterns and regularities which betrayed the underlying structure. It is this quality, the power of seeing order in apparent confusion, that has marked the work of all great men.

In addition, Ventris conforms to the general attitude of geniuses to their school days. He was above average, but not excellent; in fact, he left school before finishing his course. He derived little inspiration from the teaching, though he did have fond memories of one teacher, who taught him classics and accidentally introduced him to Linear B on a school expedition to a London exhibition on the Minoan world. And he was not interested in group activities, such as team sports, preferring to remain solitary and detached.

Can formal education ever instil this kind of exceptional creativity? Not on the evidence of past geniuses. After his retirement, the psychologist Hans Eysenck offered the following parting shot at the academic system in his study *Genius: The Natural History of Creativity*:

> The best service we can do to creativity is to let it bloom unhindered, to remove all impediments, and cherish it whenever and wherever we encounter it. We probably cannot train it, but we can prevent it from being suffocated by rules, regulations, and envious mediocrity.

Unfortunately, very few educational institutions or national governments, for all their efforts and claims to foster excellence and innovation, manage to take this lesson to heart and put it into practice in schools and universities.

# Chapter 4
# Intelligence and creativity

The fundamental reason why exceptional creativity and genius tend to elude institutional training is that they arise from many elements, such as motivation and personality, whereas schools, colleges, and universities focus chiefly on only one element: intelligence. Whatever intelligence consists of – and there is still no consensus after a century of intelligence testing – it does not appear to be the same as creativity. Intellectual skills (verbal, mathematical, and logical) and artistic creativity surely do not mutually exclude each other, but neither do they necessarily accompany each other. Indeed, as the psychologist Robert Sternberg points out in his *Handbook of Creativity*, different researchers have argued from the available evidence for five different possible relationships between intelligence and creativity: creativity as a subset of intelligence; intelligence as a subset of creativity; creativity and intelligence as overlapping sets; creativity and intelligence as coincident sets (in other words, essentially the same thing); creativity and intelligence as disjoint sets (that is, unrelated to each other).

It would be intriguing to know the intelligence quotients of a large sample of past and present geniuses when they were still unknown, in their teenage years. Would the IQ of the brilliant school student Curie be far higher than the IQ of the dull student Darwin? Would the speculative Einstein have an IQ ahead of, or behind, Curie's? Would the unschooled but polymathic Leonardo da Vinci have a low or a high IQ? What about the prodigious but narrowly focused Mozart? And the highly articulate but wholly unscientific Virginia Woolf? Of course, there are no IQ data for these people, since IQ testing began only in the 1910s; but this has not stopped certain psychologists from making estimates.

In 1917, Lewis Terman, inspired by Francis Galton's *Hereditary Genius*, attempted to calculate the IQ of Galton himself. The first volume of a four-volume biography of Galton by Karl Pearson had appeared in 1914, soon after Galton's death at the age of 89 in 1911, giving Terman ample information about the childhood and youth of his subject, up to his marriage in 1853.

Terman was particularly struck by a letter written by the child Francis on 15 February 1827, the day before his fifth birthday. It was addressed to his sister Adèle, then aged about 17, who had been his devoted teacher from his earliest childhood:

> My dear Adèle,
> I am four years old and I can read any English book. I can say all the Latin Substantives and Adjectives and active verbs besides 52 lines of Latin poetry. I can cast up any sum in addition and can multiply by 2, 3, 4, 5, 6, 7, 8, [9], 10, [11].
> I can also say the pence table. I read French a little and I know the Clock.
>
> FRANCIS GALTON.<br>Febuary-15-1827

'The only misspelling is in the date', wrote Terman. 'The numbers 9 and 11 are bracketed above, because little Francis, evidently feeling that he had claimed too much, had scratched out one of these numbers with a knife and pasted some paper over the other!'

Other relevant information from Pearson's book included the following. At the age of twelve months, Francis knew his capital letters, and six months later his alphabet; aged two and a half, he could read a little book, *Cobwebs to Catch Flies*; before he was three, he could sign his name. In his fourth year, according to his mother, he wrote and spelled correctly, without assistance, a simple letter to an uncle (reproduced by Pearson). That his reading was more than merely mechanical was shown when he was five: a school friend asked Francis's advice on what he should write in a letter to his mother about his father, who was apparently in danger of being shot over some political affair, and Francis immediately quoted Sir Walter Scott's lines: 'And if I live to be a man,/ My Father's death revenged shall be'. At the age of six, he was thoroughly familiar with Homer's *Iliad* and *Odyssey*; was reading Shakespeare's works for pleasure; and was able to repeat a page by heart after reading it twice over. At seven, he was collecting insects, shells, and minerals, then classifying and studying them in a more than childish way – a strong hint of his adult preoccupations. Later, aged thirteen, he created a series of drawings of a passenger-carrying flying machine with large flapping wings powered by some kind of steam engine, which he called 'Francis Galton's Aerostatic Project'.

Reading at the age of three – compared with the normal age of six – is equivalent to an IQ of six divided by three then multiplied by 100 (the average, or base, IQ, by definition), which gives an IQ of 200. The normal age for classification and analysis of a collection is twelve or thirteen, which implies an IQ of around 180, given that Galton was classifying and analysing insects and minerals aged seven. After comparing all of Galton's precocious behaviours with the normal mental ages for such behaviour, Terman concluded that he could estimate 'with considerable assurance' a minimum IQ for Galton that would account for the facts in Pearson's biography. 'This was unquestionably in the neighbourhood of 200, a figure not equalled by more than one child in 50,000 of the generality.'

Later, supervising his doctoral student Catharine Cox, Terman extended this initial study of historical genius, in tandem with his famous long-term study of gifted children launched at Stanford University in 1921. In 1926, Cox published an 850-page book under the title *The Early Mental Traits of Three Hundred Geniuses*. It covers not only the sciences and the arts, but also many other walks of life, such as philosophy, statesmanship, and military leadership, having a marked intellectual element.

In the 1990s, the psychologists Dean Keith Simonton, Kathleen Taylor, and Vincent Cassandro called Cox's study 'one of the classic historiometric inquiries', and Hans Eysenck lauded it as 'the only proper study of the field', a 'classic work [that] has been cited more frequently perhaps than any other book on genius'. Others from outside psychology, such as Stephen Jay Gould in his study of intelligence testing, *The Mismeasure of Man*, were scathing, however; Gould dubbed Cox's book 'a primary curiosity within a literature already studded with absurdity'.

Cox and her colleagues faced more constraints than Terman's single study of Galton. Few of her chosen individuals had lives as completely documented as Galton's. So little could she discover about Shakespeare's life that he had to be excluded. Living individuals were deliberately excluded, so there is no Curie or Einstein, no George Bernard Shaw or William Butler Yeats in the study, for instance. In addition, Cox chose to eliminate those born before 1450, along with all aristocrats, and anyone else whose achievements could not be attributed to them without dispute. All this was understandable. But some of the other omissions were hard to defend: among the scientists, no Jean-François Champollion, Carl Gauss, Robert Hooke, August Kekulé, Charles Lyell, James Clerk Maxwell, Dimitri Mendeleev, Louis Pasteur, or Christopher Wren; among the artists, no Gian Lorenzo Bernini, Johannes Brahms, Paul Cézanne, Anton Chekhov, Francisco Goya, Franz Schubert, Percy Bysshe Shelley, Leo Tolstoy, or Oscar Wilde.

The nearly 300 subjects who remain break down into the following groups: 39 scientists (including Newton), 13 visual artists (including Leonardo), 11 composers (including Mozart), 22 philosophers (including Immanuel Kant), 95 men of letters (including Byron), 27 soldiers (including Oliver Cromwell), 43 statesmen (including Abraham Lincoln), 9 revolutionary statesmen (including Robespierre), and 23 religious leaders (including Martin Luther).

Having combed biographies and other documentary sources for data, Cox ended up with dossiers totalling 6,000 pages of typed material. These she and her co-workers used to rate both intelligence and personality characteristics, and make comparisons between the various groups. Two intelligence ratings per individual were calculated: an A1 IQ for the period up to the age of 17, and an A2 IQ for the period between 17 and 26 years old. The A1 IQ was based on the subject's mastery of universal tasks such as speaking, reading, and writing, and on school performance, plus evidence of distinctive childhood achievements of the kind reported in Pearson's biography of Galton. The A2 IQ relied chiefly on the subject's academic record and early professional career. The personality profiles were created mainly by rating each subject with respect to 67 traits, using a 7-point scale.

Five co-workers, including Terman, carried out the IQ rating by independently reading the dossiers and assigning a score for each individual. But when Cox compared their five sets of scores, she found that only three of the assessors agreed substantially; the other two awarded an IQ either well above, or well below, the IQ of the first three. Arguing that these consistently high and low scores would have cancelled each other out, she controversially decided to omit them altogether and depend entirely on three, rather than five, ratings. According to her final IQ averages for each group, the soldiers had the lowest IQs (A1 IQ 115/A2 IQ 125), the philosophers the highest IQs (147/156). Visual artists and scientists fell in between, with visual artists (IQ 122/135) lower than scientists (IQ 135/152). On this basis, all but the soldiers would rank as 'gifted' (with an A2 IQ above 130). Darwin was rated at IQ 135/140, Leonardo at IQ 135/150, Michelangelo at IQ 145/160, Mozart at IQ 150/155, and Newton at IQ 130/170. The highest rating was given to John Stuart Mill at IQ 190/170.

Even the most sympathetic critics today stress that not too much weight should be placed on the individual IQs and the group averages. 'There is no question that the Cox study was carefully and conscientiously done, and is of great importance for every student of the subject', writes Eysenck. 'Yet it is imperative to resist the temptation to take the actual figures too seriously.' As he neutrally comments: 'the more data are available, the higher is the IQ estimate'. This is why, for every group, and for most individuals, the A2 IQ is higher than the A1 IQ: fully 40 points higher for Newton, whose childhood is obscure. Inevitably, there is more information available about the later than about the earlier period of a genius's life.

Faraday, too, was awarded an A1 IQ of 105 (derived from two ratings of 110 and one of 100), by virtue of slim reports about his 'faithfulness' as an errand boy and that he was a 'great questioner' when young, set against the otherwise silent background of his humble parentage and limited formal education. But this low rating for Faraday's early years jumps to an A2 IQ of 150 for his young adult years, simply because much more information is available after his employment, aged 21, at the Royal Institution by Humphry Davy. Cox openly admitted the incompleteness of the data on Faraday, and many others – such as Napoleon Bonaparte's great general Jean-André Masséna (A1 IQ a mere 100, as opposed to 135 for Napoleon himself) – but this admission does nothing to increase confidence in the validity of her IQ ratings as a whole. One must assume that she omitted Shakespeare mainly because her method would have forced her to award the Bard a below-average IQ (less than 100).

There is no answering this fundamental criticism of Cox's approach. She herself was aware of it: 'It appears that all of the IQ ratings are probably too low...and that the *true* IQ for the group...is distinctly above the estimated ratings of this study, since the estimated ratings are dependent upon data whose unreliability introduces a constant reduction of the estimated IQ from its true value.' Cox attempted to 'correct' the scores obtained from her three co-workers by adjusting them upwards to take account of missing information for certain individuals. Her correction pushed the average A1 IQ for all groups up from 135 to 152, and the average A2 IQ up from 145 to 166. But she offered no convincing rationale for these higher figures, which look more like the results of a 'fudge factor': a somewhat desperate strategy to correlate high IQ with exceptional creativity, than a scientific argument.

The truth is that insufficient information exists to allot IQs to historical geniuses. It is certainly not accurate to claim of Cox's study, in the 1986 words of the *American Journal of Psychology*, that: 'The net result was a clear demonstration that whatever other factors may have entered into the achievement of eminence, high IQ was indubitably present for those whose careers lay in statesmanship, literature, philosophy, the fine arts, and sciences – though not in the military realm.' If, for the sake of argument, we take 'high IQ' to be any IQ above about 135 (the threshold chosen by Terman), then Cox's study shows that roughly as many of her geniuses fell below this figure in the period up to age 17 as rose above it, since her average (uncorrected) A1 IQ is 135. And even this conclusion assumes that her IQ ratings are reliable and her individuals well chosen – neither of which assumption is really warranted.

A more accurate statement would be that the net result of Cox's formidable assemblage of data and its analysis is that we know that almost all geniuses, other than military ones, have an IQ well above average (100) – but that to have an IQ well above average is no guarantee of genius. Whilst this result is not too surprising, it does give the lie to the most common expectation about geniuses:

that they must by definition be extremely intelligent. After all, the American physicist Richard Feynman is generally considered an almost archetypal late 20th-century scientific genius, not just in the United States but wherever in the world physics is studied. Yet, Feynman's school-measured IQ, reported by him as 125, was not especially high (10 points short of 135, Cox's A1 IQ average). By contrast, Galton, Terman's favourite psychologist, was reckoned by him to have had a truly astonishing IQ (200). However, neither Cox and Terman, nor Galton's fellow Victorians, nor Galton's latest biographer, Nicholas Gillham, rated Galton a genius.

If a high score on an intelligence test is a poor predictor of genius, a high score on a creativity test is even less reliable at predicting exceptional creativity. Creativity tests of the kind devised by psychologists since the 1950s, mainly in the United States, aim to test divergent or lateral thinking, as opposed to

7. Richard Feynman lecturing, 1965. Though universally acknowledged as a genius in physics, Feynman had an unremarkable IQ

the convergent or logical thinking of intelligence tests. There are always many 'correct' answers to an item in a divergent thinking test, not just the single right answer to be deduced by logical methods usually expected in a convergent thinking test. Instead of posing a problem and asking the subject to converge on one answer – by selecting the correct word, number, or drawing from a set of multiple-choice solutions, the prototypical divergent thinking test requests, say: as many uses as possible for a paper clip, a range of titles for a story, or an unspecified number of plausible interpretations of an abstract line drawing. In other words, the tests search for the ability to show originality and imagination, as determined, of course, by the testers. An individual is judged to be 'creative', psychometrically speaking, if he or she can consistently produce a spectrum of divergent responses to a request, of which a proportion are markedly different from the responses of other individuals. But not *too* different, otherwise they are not recognizable as answers to the request.

Three or four decades of creativity testing – frequently with student volunteers at colleges and universities – have revealed several conclusions of note. Encouragingly, the tests are reliable. That is, if someone takes the same divergent thinking test twice, he or she will generally have a similar score; and the score will correlate significantly with his or her score on other divergent thinking tests. This is also true of convergent thinking tests. Less encouragingly, at least for creativity testers, measures of convergent and divergent thinking do not correlate well. To be more precise, according to one researcher, Frank Barron of the Institute of Personality Assessment and Research at the University of California at Berkeley, writing in 1963:

> Over the total range of intelligence and creativity a low positive correlation, probably in the neighbourhood of 0.40, obtains; beyond an IQ of about 120, however, measured intelligence is a negligible factor in creativity, and the motivational and stylistic

variables upon which our own research has laid such stress are the major determinants of creativity.

Least encouragingly of all, there is no correlation between high scorers on divergent thinking tests and their creativity in real life – in distinct contrast with the track record of convergent intelligence tests in predicting scholastic achievement at school and university and successful careers in many professional occupations, such as academic research, government, the police, and the armed forces.

Barron's conclusion, with its suggestion of an 'ability threshold' in IQ beyond which more ability is irrelevant to creativity, is controversial among psychologists. Critics include David Lubinski and Camilla Benbow, co-directors of a long-running project, the Study of Mathematically Precocious Youth (SMPY), founded in 1971, which aims to complete a 50-year longitudinal study of five cohorts, consisting of over 5,000 'intellectually talented individuals', identified over a 25-year period (1972–97). The careers of their subjects show a strong correlation between a score on a standardized intelligence test sat at the age of 12 and the later earning of a doctorate, a high income, a tenured position at a high-ranking US university, and patents. 'That a two-hour test can identify twelve-year-olds who will earn this ultimate educational credential [a doctorate] at 50 times base-rate expectations is remarkable', noted Lubinski and Benbow in 2006. 'To be sure, factors other than ability level are important,' they concluded. 'Nevertheless, other things being equal, more ability is always better.' Terman's earlier long-term study of gifted children supports the Lubinski/Benbow conclusion.

But whilst such studies reveal a connection between increasing intelligence and increasing achievement, they tell us nothing about increasing intelligence and exceptional creativity or genius. The award of a scholarship or fellowship, a respected academic position, a patent or a prize – with the possible exception of the Nobel prize and a few other highly prestigious international prizes – is not by itself an apt measure of exceptional creativity. The individuals in the SMPY are still comparatively young, but the signs of greatness in their future achievements are not conspicuous in the SMPY's published results. Terman's half-century older study does not give grounds for optimism. None of his gifted students, for all their considerable worldly success as a group, achieved anywhere near 'genius' in any field, as Joel Shurkin (a Pulitzer prize-winning journalist) makes abundantly clear in his study *Terman's Kids*. None won a Pulitzer prize or a Nobel prize, for example; moreover, Terman's initial IQ tests rejected the future Nobel laureate William Shockley, one of the inventors of the transistor, after twice testing him, as it also did another future Nobel laureate in physics, Luis Alvarez.

But the chief difficulty in linking intelligence with creativity and genius is more theoretical than experimental. Psychologists may be able to measure intelligence, but ever since Galton's day, they have been unable to agree on even an approximate definition of the concept.

Back in 1921 – as Terman was launching his study of gifted children, Cox was beginning her research on historical geniuses, and IQ tests were about to take hold of American schools – the *Journal of Educational Psychology* published a symposium, 'Intelligence and Its Measurement', in which fourteen experts were invited to define their conceptions of intelligence. Five did not address the issue directly in their replies. Of the other nine answers, Terman's stood out from the rest. He said intelligence was 'the ability to carry on abstract thinking': a surprisingly narrow definition from someone interested in linking intelligence with genius. A second psychologist favoured 'the capacity for knowledge, and knowledge possessed'. The other seven answers perhaps had more in common: they all involved the capacity to learn from experience, and adaptation to one's environment. None, though, mentioned any connection between intelligence and creativity. With the possible exception of Terman's idea of abstract thinking, the experts' emphasis was firmly on intelligence as something reactive, rather than creative.

Almost a century later, the diversity of views about intelligence persists. 'Innumerable tests are available for measuring intelligence, yet no one is quite certain of what intelligence is, or even of just what it is that the available tests are measuring', wrote Sternberg in 1987. Another well-known researcher, James Flynn, admits this, too. But his own beguiling book, *What Is Intelligence?*, published in 2007, does not clarify the confusion very much. Flynn compares the debate over the nature of intelligence to the old debate in physics about the nature of light, settled (sort of) by the advent of quantum theory and the concept of wave-particle duality. Flynn writes:

> Much time was wasted before it was realized that light could act like a wave in certain of its manifestations and like a stream of particles in other manifestations. We have to realize that intelligence can act like a highly correlated set of abilities on one level and like a set of functionally independent abilities on other levels.

These levels are: the brain's neural clusters, individual differences in performance, and society. This sounds promising, but then Flynn adds, honestly if not too helpfully: 'We are a long way from integrating what is known on these three levels into one body of theory.'

Flynn's research does offer some clues, though. It cannot tell us anything directly about exceptional creativity, but it sheds new light on the slippery concept of IQ, and why it caused Cox so much trouble in her study. It may also explain why Feynman's IQ, measured around 1930, was rather lower than we might have expected for so brilliant an intellect.

In the mid-1980s, Flynn discovered an astonishing and subversive fact about mean IQ figures, which was soon widely accepted and later dubbed the 'Flynn effect' by other psychologists. In the post-war decades, mean IQ had trended steadily upwards – not just in one or two countries, but in all developed countries where sufficient IQ data were available, including the United States, Britain, Belgium, the Netherlands, Norway, Israel, and Argentina. Over the second half of the century, some two generations, mean IQ had grown by almost 20 points in the United States and Europe. Other, less reliable, data suggested that the growth went back to 1900, and that the mean IQ in 1900, scored against current norms, would have been somewhere between 50 and 70 – in other words, mentally retarded.

The picture is further complicated by the fact that the rise is not equally spread among the various components of intelligence tests that are averaged together to give a single IQ: the changes in different abilities do not correlate well. Essentially, without going into details, young people have become much smarter on tests that measure the ability to compare and classify concepts, whether in words or pictures, but they have shown almost no improvement in their vocabulary, general knowledge, and arithmetical ability. Between 1947 and 2002, Americans gained 24 points on tests for the first skill, 4 points on vocabulary tests, and just 2 points on general knowledge and arithmetic tests.

All this was wholly unexpected, because IQ tests are normalized by testing an age cohort at regular intervals, in order that the mean IQ will remain the same from generation to generation. Without such normalization, some individuals will receive obsolete tests and be compared not with their contemporaries but with a previous generation. The puzzling rise in mean IQ suggests that, in Flynn's words: 'Either the children of today [are] far brighter than their parents or, at least in some circumstances, IQ tests [are] not good measures of intelligence.'

His tantalizing discovery has generated a lot of discussion, and there is, as yet, no consensus on the reason for the rise in mean IQ. Obviously, more and more children went on from school to college and university in the 20th century, which must have some relevance to IQ. Also evident is that each new generation acquires skills, such as computing, that challenge the intelligence of their parents. Undoubtedly, too, there has been a continuing rise in the amount of information available to the average person, which may have affected abilities that form part of intelligence. 'The ability to improve working memory through training might well be the key to understanding the entire Flynn effect', speculates the neuroscientist Torkel Klingberg in *The Overflowing Brain*. Flynn himself puts the rise in IQ mainly down to what he calls increasing adoption of 'scientific spectacles', which allow us to compare and classify concepts easily.

> During the 20th century, people invested their intelligence in the solution of new cognitive problems. Formal education played a proximate causal role but a full appreciation of causes involves grasping the total impact of the industrial revolution.

To express the issue raised by Flynn another way, it appears that Feynman's school-tested IQ (*c.* 1930) might have been more like 150–55, rather than 125, were he to have been tested today. As for the geniuses in Cox's study, such as Leonardo and Faraday, who belong to the period before 1900, their 'fossil' IQs would seem to have required correction for rather more than just Cox's lack of information about their early years. 'We are no wiser than Aristotle was', noted Martin Rees, the president of Britain's Royal Society, in 2010; it is our technical advances that make us seem more intelligent than our ancestors. The debate about the relationship between high intelligence and exceptional creativity continues to churn.

# Chapter 5
# Genius and madness

The connection between genius and mental illness is paradoxically clearer and murkier than that between genius and high intelligence. Vincent van Gogh, perhaps the most celebrated example of a genius who was mentally ill, suffered from severe depression, mutilated one of his ears in 1888, entered an asylum, and shot himself in 1890 at the age of 37 whilst painting at the height of his creative powers; indeed, his greatest work dates from the last two years of his life. Almost unrecognized in Van Gogh's lifetime, his paintings were gradually accepted as works of high artistic importance and are now among the most recognized images in world art. His periodic mental derangement was never in doubt, either by himself or his family and associates. Yet neither was his sanity, as proved by his extensive, detailed, and rational letters to his art dealer brother Theo and fellow artists like Émile Bernard and Paul Gauguin. 'His output of letters and pictures displays a strong internal cohesion', three researchers at the Van Gogh Museum in Amsterdam wrote in 2010. 'This double *oeuvre* cannot be dismissed as the product of a sick mind. On the contrary, it can only be seen as the legacy of a truly great intellect: the real Van Gogh.' But despite decades of forensic study, the fascinating coexistence of his mental illness and his exceptional creativity remains difficult to explain, while exerting an extraordinary grip on our contemporary imagination.

8. *Self-Portrait with Bandaged Ear*, painting by Vincent van Gogh, 1889

The idea of a connection has a long and lusty history. In ancient Greece, Aristotle (or his pupil Theophrastus) asked: 'Why is it that all men who are outstanding in philosophy, poetry, or the arts are melancholic?' As examples, Aristotle cited Homeric, Sophoclean, and mythological heroes like Ajax and Bellerophon, and historical figures such as the philosophers Empedocles, Plato, and Socrates.

(According to legend, Empedocles died by throwing himself into the crater of Mount Etna, seeking divine status.)

Aristotle's view influenced Renaissance thinkers. In the 15th century, the Florentine Neoplatonic philosopher Marsilio Ficino saw melancholy as 'the corporeal price, as it were, to be paid for the soul's "heroic" endeavour to traverse the rationally unbridgeable gulf separating finite and transient nature from infinite and eternal supernature', writes Noel Brann in *The Debate over the Origin of Genius during the Italian Renaissance*. Shakespeare in *A Midsummer Night's Dream* intuited something similar. 'The lunatic, the lover, and the poet/ Are of imagination all compact', says Theseus, the king. 'One sees more devils than vast hell can hold;/ That is the madman. The lover, all as frantic,/ Sees Helen's beauty in a brow of Egypt./ The poet's eye, in a fine frenzy rolling,/ Doth glance from heaven to earth, from earth to heaven'. Theseus concludes: 'Such tricks hath strong imagination,…'.

In the 19th century, at the time of the Romantic movement, the lives and works of Byron and Robert Schumann – both of them self-destructive – came to epitomize a link between mental illness and genius, which Van Gogh then reinforced. In the 20th century, three of America's leading artistic figures, Ernest Hemingway, Sylvia Plath, and Jackson Pollock, took their own lives as a result of depression – and so, in Britain, did Virginia Woolf.

Scientists as a group have suffered less from mental illness. Nonetheless, a 1990s survey by the psychiatrist Felix Post based on the biographies of 291 exceptionally creative individuals came to the conclusion that, judged by modern diagnostic standards, Einstein and Faraday suffered from 'mild' psychopathology, Darwin and Pasteur from 'marked' psychopathology, and Bohr and Galton from 'severe' psychopathology, along with a number of other major scientists. Darwin, for example, endured decades of unexplained illness, which seems to have been caused by his anxiety about the public reception of his theory of natural selection.

The dramatic stories told about individual geniuses tend to distort the overall picture of mental illness and creativity. Anecdotes can easily give the impression that mental instability is a *sine qua non* of exceptional creativity; a notion that is perhaps nourished by the average person's desire to explain away exceptionally creative achievement. For every such example, however, it is not difficult to find a counter-example of an exceptionally creative artist or scientist in a similar field who shows none of the symptoms of psychopathology.

Only by studying the mental health of substantial groups, whether of past or of living highly creative individuals, can psychologists try to reach a valid conclusion about whether Aristotle's observation was correct or not. We shall examine three studies of different types of artistic creativity from three different periods: fine artists in the Italian Renaissance during the 14th to 16th centuries; British poets during the age of Romanticism in the 18th to 19th centuries; and American writers in the second half of the 20th century.

The Renaissance has canonical status as one of the greatest flowerings of creativity in history. Nonetheless, the period gives the impression of a dearth, rather than an excess, of psychopathology among artists, especially when compared to the equally canonical Romantic period. Whilst key Renaissance artists like Botticelli, Brunelleschi, Leonardo, Raphael, and Titian undoubtedly come down to us as strong personalities, they do not appear to have regarded themselves as isolated, tortured geniuses having a tendency towards self-destruction, with the possible exception of Michelangelo; in fact, only one of them, the lesser painter Rosso Fiorentino, was reported to have committed suicide, and this report has subsequently been disproved.

The psychologist Andrew Steptoe investigated the personalities of Renaissance artists by analysing the biographies presented in Giorgio Vasari's classic *Lives of the Most Excellent Painters, Sculptors, and Architects*, first published in Italian in the middle decades of the 16th century. 'Did he see the most creative individuals as disturbed, melancholic, and unconventional, or in other terms?' Steptoe asked himself.

Vasari's book is divided into three parts, covering early, middle-period, and contemporary artists. The information in part one – up to about 1400 – is generally accepted to be very unreliable, given the paucity of facts available to Vasari. Steptoe's study therefore excludes part one of Vasari's work and confines itself to the biographies in parts two and three, covering 123 later artists – that is, 83 painters, 38 sculptors, and 22 architects (many individuals having more than one craft) – who include the best-known figures of the Renaissance.

There is also the problem of Vasari's personal reliability. His factual errors have long been known. But these matter less in a study of personality than the question of his point of view: whether or not he selected from and sanitized his sources to create a picture in line with his underlying agenda that artists were professionals, not mere artisans, worthy of the respect accorded to established professions such as the law, the church, and medicine. There is some evidence that he did. On the other hand, sufficient eccentricities and undesirable traits are mentioned in the *Lives* to suggest that the biographies can be taken mainly at face value. Even Vasari's favourite artists were 'just as likely to be tarred with negative attributes such as pride or fecklessness as the other artists', writes Steptoe. Also significant is the fact that the biographies were taken seriously, not sceptically, by Vasari's contemporaries, who themselves knew much about the artists he described.

Steptoe scrutinized the biographies for references to each of 42 different characteristics, including general traits such as honesty and pride, along with features such as melancholy and eccentricity, which are widely thought to form part of an 'artistic temperament'. Inevitably, the material available did not always prove accommodating to his imposed lines of enquiry, and so Steptoe eventually adopted 13 broader categories of commentary by Vasari on an artist's character suggesting: high ability; studiousness; capacity for hard work; negative criticism; sociability; courteousness; sophistication; moderation; unworldliness; depressiveness; eccentricity; unworthiness; and conceitedness.

The most common trait turns out to be studiousness – found in 48 out of the 123 artists (39 per cent). The next most common is courteousness (at 31 per cent). Depressive tendencies and eccentricities are relatively uncommon, as are sophistication and unworldliness. 'There is little here to endorse the presence either of a melancholic temperament, or of the hypersensitive alienated creature of modern conceptualizations', notes Steptoe. Perhaps, though, these characteristics may have been a feature of the elite minority of truly great artists, in other words the subset of painters, sculptors, and architects judged by Vasari to have exceptionally high ability? Not so: after Steptoe has separated out this group and repeated the analysis, the initial pattern becomes even more evident. The elite group is seen to be more studious, courteous, sociable, and moderate in its habits than the majority of the artists, with no higher incidence of depressive tendencies or eccentric behaviour. And after Steptoe has repeated the analysis with the still more select group of 11 artists known to be Vasari's favourites (Masaccio, Brunelleschi, Donatello, Leonardo, Raphael, Andrea del Sarto, Rosso Fiorentino, Giulio Romano, Perino del Vaga, Francesco Salviati, and Michelangelo), the pattern becomes yet more pronounced. It appears that the greatest artists of the Renaissance were neither notably unconventional nor notably temperamental, but on the contrary studious, hard-working, courteous, sociable, and sophisticated. This is indeed how Leonardo appears to art historians during the period of the 1480s to 1490s, when he worked at the court of the duke of Milan and painted *The Last Supper* – apart perhaps from his well-known failure to finish most of his works.

'If this was the case, then psychological disturbance, unconventionality, or other aspects of the "artistic personality" cannot be intrinsic to creativity', concludes Steptoe. In Renaissance Italy, these attributes presumably did not aid an artist's struggle to achieve a dependable income and social respect. From the late 18th century onwards, by contrast, they seem to have conformed better to social expectations of the artist and thereby helped to generate and maintain public interest in art.

A second biographical survey, this time of 36 British and Irish poets born between 1705 and 1805, suggests an utterly different relationship between psychopathology and creativity. 'It can be seen that a strikingly high rate of mood disorders, suicide, and institutionalization occurred within this group of poets and their families', writes the psychiatrist Kay Redfield Jamison, who conducted the survey, in *Touched with Fire: Manic-Depressive Illness and the Artistic Temperament.*

The group embraces all of the standard names of the period – William Blake, Robert Burns, Lord Byron, John Clare, Samuel Taylor Coleridge, William Cowper, Thomas Gray, John Keats, Walter Scott, Percy Bysshe Shelley, William Wordsworth, and others – as well as less well-known poets like Leigh Hunt, James Clarence Mangan, and Joanna Baillie. Although the sample size was much smaller than Steptoe's, the sources for research on the poets were more plentiful than for the artists, since they included letters, medical records, and family histories, in addition to biographical works, and of course the poets' published works. These were examined for symptoms and patterns of depression, mania, hypomania, and mixed states, taking into account other psychiatric or medical illnesses (for example, Keats's tuberculosis) that might confuse a diagnosis.

Jamison diagnoses Scott as a possible sufferer from recurrent depression. She notes:

> At various times described himself as suffering from a 'disposition to causeless alarm – much lassitude – and decay of vigour and intellect', a *morbus eruditorum* [scholars' disease], and a 'black dog' of melancholy.

Byron, she thinks, almost certainly suffered from manic depression (bipolar disorder):

> Recurrent, often agitated, melancholia. Volatile temperament with occasional 'paroxysms of rage'. Mercurial and extravagant; worsening depressions over time. Strong family history of mental instability and suicide.

She quotes Scott's powerful letter about his great friend Byron:

> There is something dreadful in reflecting that one gifted so much above his fellow-creatures, should thus labour under some strange mental malady that destroys his peace of mind and happiness, altho' it cannot quench the fire of his genius.

Two of the 36 poets – Thomas Chatterton and Thomas Lovell Beddoes – committed suicide. Six, including Clare and Cowper, were committed to lunatic asylums or madhouses. More than half of the 36 showed strong evidence of mood disorders, like Byron. Jamison's comparisons of the group with the mental illness of the general population of the period show that the poets were more than five times as likely to have committed suicide, at least 20 times more likely to have been committed to an asylum or madhouse, and 30 times more likely to have suffered from manic-depressive illness. This latter group includes, in addition to Byron, Blake, Coleridge, and Shelley. Only 7 out of the 36 poets – fewer than one-quarter – show no indication of a significant mood disorder, and they are not among the most celebrated.

Our third survey involves 20th-century writers, and was the first scientific attempt to diagnose the relationship between creativity and psychopathology in living writers. Over several years, beginning in the early 1970s, the psychiatrist Nancy Andreasen (originally a professor of Renaissance literature) conducted structured interviews, based on systematic psychiatric diagnostic criteria, with writers in residence at the established and respected Iowa Writers' Workshop. She also interviewed a control group whose occupations did not require high levels of creativity, matched for education and age with the writers. Each person was interviewed separately, not in a group. Initially, there were 15 writers and 15 controls, but this group later expanded to a total of 30 writers and 30 controls – just short of the 36 dead poets studied by Jamison. Needless to say, the interviewed writers (who remain anonymous in the published study) were not at the exceptional level of Jamison's poets. However, some had received national acclaim in the United States, whilst others were graduate students or teaching fellows of the workshop. (Iowa Workshop graduates have won 16 Pulitzer prizes since 1947; faculty members have included John Berryman, John Cheever, Robert Lowell, and Philip Roth.)

Andreasen began with a working hypothesis that the writers would be generally healthy, psychologically speaking, but have a higher incidence of schizophrenia in their family than the control group. She was aware from reliable studies of adopted children born to mothers with schizophrenia compared to the adopted children born to mentally normal mothers, that schizophrenia was known to be inherited; 10 per cent of the adopted children of schizophrenic mothers are themselves schizophrenic, despite growing up in a normal environment, as compared to an incidence of schizophrenia in the general population of less than 1 per cent. Moreover, inherited schizophrenia was evident to Andreasen in the families of Einstein, James Joyce, and Bertrand Russell. It had been reported, too, by an Icelandic psychiatrist among the relatives of successful individuals listed in Iceland's *Who's Who*.

The general opinion among psychiatrists in the early 1970s was that the genetic tendency towards schizophrenia might express itself either in a severe form, as an illness, or in a mild form, as creativity.

However, Andreasen's interviews showed that not a single one of the 30 Iowa Workshop writers had any of the symptoms of schizophrenia. Instead, the majority – 80 per cent, as compared to 30 per cent of the control group – met her formal diagnostic criteria for a major mood disorder: either bipolar illness or unipolar depression. (The percentage in the control group is surprisingly high, given the typical percentage for the general population, which is between 5 per cent and 8 per cent.) Most of these writers had received treatment, in the form of hospitalization, or outpatient medication, or psychotherapy. She also found a significantly higher incidence of mood disorders and creativity in the first-degree relatives (parents and siblings) of the writers, than among the first-degree relatives of the controls.

Looking back on her pioneering study in 2005, Andreasen felt that it confirmed 'two apparently conflicting, but prevailing, ideas about the nature of creativity and its relationship to mental illness'. The first, espoused by Terman in his Stanford study of gifted children, is that gifted people are in fact 'super-normal'. The same might be said of the Renaissance artists in Steptoe's study (far more creative though they were than Terman's subjects). 'My writers certainly were... charming, fun, articulate, and disciplined' writes Andreasen.

> They typically followed very similar schedules, getting up in the morning and allocating a large chunk of time to writing during the earlier part of the day. They would rarely let a day go by without writing. In general, they had a close relationship with friends and family.

But on the other hand, like the dead poets in Jamison's study, the writers also manifested a view of madness and creativity similar to Shakespeare's in *A Midsummer Night's Dream*.

> Many definitely had experienced periods of significant mood disorder. Importantly, though handicapping creativity when they occurred, these periods of mood disorder were not permanent or long-lived.

Moreover, the mood disorders could possibly be productive.

> In some instances, they may even have provided powerful material upon which the writer could later draw, as a Wordsworthian 'emotion recollected in tranquillity'.

Creative individuals are generally ambivalent about this last notion. None has claimed to be able to produce work of enduring value when seriously depressed. But few have wished to be entirely free of their demons, fearing their own sterility. Their attitude towards their mental illness is, not surprisingly, complex. Whilst they are under no illusion that their illness produces their creativity, they suspect that it is an inseparable companion that must be accepted if not welcomed.

The early 20th-century poet Rainer Maria Rilke famously said: 'If my demons leave me, I am afraid my angels may take flight as well.' When the artist Edvard Munch (painter of *The Scream*) was told that psychiatric treatment could rid him of many of his troubles, he responded: 'They are part of me and my art. They are indistinguishable from me, and it would destroy my art. I want to keep those sufferings.' The Nobel prize-winning mathematician and economist John Nash, whose paranoid schizophrenia became the subject of the book and movie *A Beautiful Mind*, when asked by an incredulous fellow mathematician 'How could you believe you are being recruited by aliens from outer space to save the world?', replied: 'Because the ideas I had about supernatural beings came to me the same way that my mathematical ideas did. So I took them seriously.' Even Einstein recognized the necessity of accepting psychological lows as well as highs in his search for a theory of general relativity, which made him gravely ill.

Before the accidental discovery of lithium salts in 1948 for treating mania, and the discovery of other drugs such as reserpine and chlorpromazine in the 1950s for controlling schizophrenia, sufferers had little choice but to come to terms with their illness. Once reliable drugs were available, creative people had to decide upon the advantages and disadvantages of taking them.

Robert Lowell took lithium in the late 1960s, and found himself both relieved from breakdown and more poetically productive. But he told the neurologist Oliver Sacks: 'my poetry has lost much of its force' – and it is true that Lowell's later poems, post-lithium, are not as highly regarded by critics as his earlier work. With others, too, there does appear to be a trade-off between quantity and quality, according to a 1979 study of artists with manic depression (bipolar disorder) who were given lithium carbonate by the psychiatrist Mogens Schou. Taking lithium can allow someone to work again, but at some cost to insights obtained during manic highs. As the poet Gwyneth Lewis (the first National Poet of Wales) remarks in an essay, 'Dark Gifts', written for the collection *Poets on Prozac*:

> Only two of my eight books have been written while taking antidepressants, so I find it very difficult to distinguish between the effect of the medication and a development of my own style away from ornamentation and towards greater simplicity (which, of all literary effects, requires the most skill and is the most difficult to achieve). Even if it was proven that antidepressants adversely affected my ability as a poet, I'd still take them. After being a zombie for months, being able to write at all is a miracle, and that

participation in the creative discipline, rather than a more objective measure of excellence, is the bottom line for me.

To psychologists, the issue of productivity versus excellence is of compelling interest for the light it sheds on the nature of genius. While mania without doubt increases productivity, might it also sometimes improve quality too? If a creative person has a sustained burst of energy and self-confidence, it would seem reasonable that this should have a positive influence on his or her work. On the other hand, mania is likely to preclude the operation of the critical faculty essential for exceptional creativity, which edits with cool detachment what has been created passionately.

In other words, simply put, does madness enhance or diminish genius? With this in mind, the psychologist Robert Weisberg analysed in two separate studies the output of two major artists: the compositions of Robert Schumann and the poems of Emily Dickinson. Both have been retrospectively diagnosed as sufferers from manic depression (bipolar disorder), though this is more certain for Schumann than for Dickinson. He attempted suicide more than once and ended his short life in a mental asylum, where he starved himself to death in 1856; Dickinson had a more conventional and somewhat longer life, but became a recluse for almost two decades before her death in 1886. Almost all of her poetry was published posthumously.

Between 1829 and 1851, Schumann more or less alternated between moods of hypomania and depression, judging from his doctors' records, his letters, the letters of those who knew him, and other historical documents. Naturally, it is not possible to diagnose his mood at all times, moreover a particular mood may also have lasted for less than a whole year. Nevertheless, a dominant mood can be established for most of the years of Schumann's creative period. The number of his compositions in each year does not track these moods exactly, but there are two peaks, in 1840 and 1849: manic years when he composed 25 or

**9. Emily Dickinson, 1848. Did mental illness benefit her poetry?**

more works – far more than in any other year. The first of these peaks, Schumann's 'year of song', corresponded with his marriage to Clara Wieck. The average number of his compositions in the years of hypomania is approximately five times the average number in the years of depression.

To assess the compositions' quality, rather than their number, Weisberg counted the number of available recordings for each composition; the more recordings there were, the higher the quality of the composition. He could have chosen other measures, such as the number of appearances of a work in concert programmes, or the assessments of experts, such as conductors, musicians, musicologists, or critics. The number of recordings per composition has the advantage that it is both convenient to measure, and correlates well with other measures, for example the frequency with which a work is discussed in critical analyses of music. Hence, the number of recordings per composition is more than simply a measure of the popularity of the composition.

'If Schumann's periods of mania improved his thought processes, then compositions produced during his manic years should be recorded more frequently, on average, than compositions produced during the depressive years', notes Weisberg. But his analysis does not support this hypothesis. The average number of recordings per composition from Schumann's manic years, taken together, is actually about the same as the average number from his depressive years, taken together. Indeed, the peak number of recordings relates to a year of depression, *not* to a manic year. The implication is that, although Schumann was highly motivated to compose in his manic years, and he therefore composed far more works at this time, his motivation did not improve the quality of his creativity.

Dickinson and her poetry were subjected by Weisberg to a similar kind of analysis of quantity and quality of poems written during manic, depressed, and neutral years, as defined by external evidence, such as Dickinson's correspondence. Most of her poems were written in an eight-year period between 1858 and 1865, when she was 28–35 years old. They fall into two four-year phases, divided by an emotional crisis. This time, the measure of quality was the number of appearances of a poem in more than a dozen compendia of poetry published during the 20th century (instead of numbers of musical recordings). As with Schumann, there are found to be large differences in quantity of poetic output, with manic years resulting in high output. Unlike Schumann, however, there is some evidence that the poems produced during manic years were of higher quality. So the results for Dickinson do not agree with those for Schumann: instead, they provide some support for the idea that mania can increase creativity, although the shorter span of Dickinson's major productivity – eight years as compared to Schumann's more than 20 years – makes the Dickinson analysis less rigorous and convincing.

To establish a definitive connection between mental illness and creativity is impossible, at present. Psychologists and psychiatrists assess it very differently. All accept, with Shakespeare, that there is something about madness that can inform our understanding of genius – especially among poets. 'It seems that the age-old notion that genius is related to madness was not entirely unfounded, even if some invalid *explanations* have been offered', writes R. Ochse in his balanced survey. Many accept that the association arises from natural selection, which must surely favour creativity as an advantageous evolutionary trait. But for now, there is no agreement on the detail of where creativity's connection with madness actually lies.

# Chapter 6
# Chameleon personalities

Is there a personality conducive to genius? The notion seems unlikely on the face of it. Even if we limit ourselves to geniuses who worked simultaneously in the same field, the most obvious pattern is their *difference* in personality. In the arts, think of Leonardo and Michelangelo, Shakespeare and Christopher Marlowe, Mozart and Joseph Haydn, Van Gogh and Gauguin, T. S. Eliot and Ezra Pound, and in the sciences Newton and Edmond Halley, Darwin and Thomas Henry Huxley, Marie Curie and Ernest Rutherford, Einstein and Bohr, Francis Crick and James Watson.

> Probably the personalities of creative people are not as diverse as are creative people themselves – that is, there probably is not a unique personality configuration for each creative person. However, there is reason to believe that there are at the very least numerous creative personalities, and it is probably true that even people working within the same subfield of the arts or the sciences can approach their work from very different perspectives, meaning that their personalities would probably be different,

comments a cautious Robert Weisberg.

The scientific study of personality was for decades a poor relation in psychology. Sigmund Freud launched it with his concepts of id, ego, and psychoanalysis, a century or so ago. Yet even Freud was dubious that psychoanalysis was a science. The terms 'extraversion' and 'introversion', basic to today's studies of personality, were introduced by Carl Jung as long ago as 1921. But during the 20th century, no particular measure of personality enjoyed anything like the agreement attaching to the measurement of intelligence by IQ.

Instead, there were as many theories and measures of personality as psychologists studying the subject. Eysenck, for instance, argued strongly from the 1950s onwards for an analysis of personality based on three dimensions: extraversion, neuroticism, and psychoticism. During this confused period, according to Daniel Nettle in his book *Personality* (2007), 'one psychologist might give you a score for Reward Dependence and Harm Avoidance, whilst another might classify you as a Thinking, Feeling, Sensing, or Intuiting type'. If personality psychology was to become a discipline, rather than being similar to the entertaining personality questionnaires in general-interest magazines, its practitioners had to establish that individuals truly did have an enduring personality in the flux of everyday life and social encounters, stable from year to year, decade to decade. Yet if this were really so, what dimensions should be used to measure and define it? How should psychologists check whether or not it endured? And how should they find out which of these dimensions were relevant to creativity?

Recently, there has been some progress in answering these questions. As a result, there is now more of a consensus in personality research, at least about the personality of ordinary people, if not very much about that of exceptional creators.

The first reason is that the so-called 'five-factor model' of personality seems to fit the evidence from studies of individuals and groups. The model appears to be 'the most comprehensive, reliable, and useful framework for discussing human personality that we have ever had', writes Nettle. Personality is now widely tested and factored along five dimensions, which are the following character traits: extraversion, neuroticism, conscientiousness, agreeableness, and openness. (These are Nettle's categories, but other psychologists use broadly similar ones.) High scorers on extraversion are, says Nettle, 'outgoing, enthusiastic', whereas low scorers are 'aloof, quiet'. High scorers on neuroticism are 'prone to stress and worry', low scorers 'emotionally stable'. High scorers on conscientiousness are 'organized, self-directed', low scorers 'spontaneous, careless'. High scorers on agreeableness are 'trusting, empathetic', low scorers 'uncooperative, hostile'. Finally – and supposedly most relevant to creativity – high scorers on openness are 'creative, imaginative, eccentric', low scorers 'practical, conventional'. These five-factor scores for ordinary individuals are found to be as constant when measured over a decade as over a week.

Other reasons for consensus come from neuroscience, genetics, and evolutionary psychology. Brain-imaging scans, which began in the 1990s, suggest that individual differences in brain structure and functioning may be mappable onto the dimensions of the five-factor model. In other words, a statement like 'X is high in extraversion' should have a biological correlate in the brain, perhaps in the mid-brain dopamine reward systems, though this has yet to be satisfactorily located. Then there is the evidence from the sequencing of the human genome, completed in 2001. Personality appears partly determined by an individual's genetic variants. For example, a study of New Zealand adults over time showed that subjects with the greatest tendency to depression – that is, high scorers on neuroticism – had two copies of short forms of the serotonin transporter genes, as opposed to either one copy of the short form and one of a long form or two copies of the long form, inherited from the subjects' parents. Lastly, there is the infusion into psychology of evolutionary thinking, from the 1980s onwards. Why should natural selection have produced human personality traits? The evolutionary explanation for the existence of a high level of neuroticism is that in earlier times highly neurotic individuals had the advantage of being better able to anticipate danger (such as being attacked by a large predator) than those with low neuroticism, despite the disadvantage to them of increased anxiety and risk of depression. Those who scored high for openness were presumably good at adaptation, at finding new and creative solutions to unfamiliar problems, while at the same time being prone to bizarre beliefs and psychosis (like John Nash in *A Beautiful Mind*).

Unfortunately for any putative 'creative personality', 'openness' is the least well analysed of the five-factor traits. Nettle calls it 'mysterious and difficult to pin down', and admits that other psychologists define it somewhat differently under labels such as 'culture' and 'intellect'. Furthermore, the convincing method to determine whether personality characteristics and creative performance are causally linked would be to take a group of young people before they show any eminence and study their personality and creativity over the course of their lives, as Terman did with intelligence. But so far there have been almost no such long-term studies.

This last limitation applies *a fortiori* to the exceptionally creative. According to Freud, 'before creativity, the psychoanalyst must lay down his arms', and 'the nature of artistic attainment is psychoanalytically inaccessible to us'. At present, personality psychology has nothing very useful to say about genius. Nettle's *Personality* is silent on the subject, for example. The only empirical study of the personality traits of creative, compared with exceptionally creative, people is the historical survey of genius carried out by Terman's student Cox – and we know from Chapter 4 how flawed that was. It also predates today's five-factor model. To compile a personality profile for a long-dead genius is likely to be an ad hoc procedure of little scientific value. Of Cox's roughly 300 geniuses, only 100 of them could be rated for personality traits, for lack of sufficient evidence.

The chief difficulty is not lack of evidence, though. In my view, it is the near-certainty that exceptionally creative people do not actually have the kind of stable personality on which the five-factor model is predicated. The more creative a person is, the more multifarious is his or her personality. An exasperated Theo van Gogh wrote of his elder brother Vincent: 'It appears as if there are two different beings in him, the one marvellously gifted, fine and delicate, the other selfish and heartless.' Thus there may be no point looking for a stable personality in an exceptionally creative individual, because it does not exist. To be exceptionally creative means to have a chameleon personality. Exceptionally creative individuals modify their personalities to suit their context.

An insightful comment on Mozart's composing by his wife Constanze illustrates this chameleon tendency.

> When some grand conception was working in his brain he was purely abstracted, walked about the apartment and knew not what was passing around, but when once arranged in his mind, he needed no Piano Forte but would take music paper and whilst he wrote would say...'Now, my dear wife, have the goodness to repeat what has been talked of', and [my] conversation never interrupted him.

A vivid eyewitness account reveals Einstein's changeable personality. Einstein never shied away from vigorous debate with friends and fellow scientists (notably arguments with Niels Bohr and Max Born concerning quantum theory), from incisive and witty press interviews, and from personal celebrity; such extraverted behaviour was among the reasons for Einstein's unique fame. But his most creative science was done in privacy and relative isolation. The account comes from two physicist collaborators of Einstein in the 1930s, Banesh Hoffmann and Leopold Infeld. Hoffmann recalled:

> Whenever we came to an impasse the three of us had heated discussions – in English for my benefit, because my German was

not too fluent – but when the argument became really intricate Einstein, without realising it, would lapse into German. He thought more readily in his native tongue. Infeld would join him in that tongue, while I struggled so hard to follow what was being said that I rarely had time to interject a remark till the excitement died down.

When it became clear, as it often did, that even resorting to German did not solve the problem, we would all pause, and then Einstein would stand up quietly and say, in his quaint English, 'I vill a little t'ink'. So saying he would pace up and down or walk around in circles, all the time twirling a lock of his long, greying hair around his forefinger. At these moments of high drama Infeld and I would remain completely still, not daring to move or make a sound, lest we interrupt his train of thought. A minute would pass in this way and another, and Infeld and I would eye each other silently while Einstein continued pacing and all the time twirling his hair. There was a dreamy, far-away, and yet sort of inward look on his face. There was no appearance at all of intense concentration. Another minute would pass and another, and then all of a sudden Einstein would visibly relax and a smile would light up his face. No longer did he pace and twirl his hair. He seemed to come back to his surroundings and to notice us once more, and then he would tell us the solution to the problem and almost always the solution worked.

The personalities of Mozart and Einstein in these vignettes do not lend themselves to easy classification using the five-factor model. Mozart would score high for extraversion ('outgoing, enthusiastic') when giving a concert performance in front of an audience or conducting one of his operas, yet low ('aloof, quiet') when composing at home. And the same would be the case for Einstein on one of his celebrity tours in the 1920s, as compared with him at home working on physics. Einstein was often said, not least by himself, to seem 'apart' from the world. 'I am truly a "lone traveller" and have never belonged to my country, my home, my friends, or even my immediate family, with my whole heart', he wrote when he was about 50. Thus, Mozart and Einstein could be extraverts – and also introverts. Any attempt to measure their degree of extraversion would necessarily suggest not a stable personality but something mercurial.

The other four traits in the model might well vary considerably for Mozart and Einstein. For conscientiousness ('organized, self-directed' versus 'spontaneous, careless') and openness to experience ('creative, imaginative, eccentric' versus 'practical, conventional'), Mozart and Einstein would tend to score high under most circumstances. However, it is worth observing that Mozart had a penchant for spontaneous improvisation during performances; that his father Leopold frequently berated him for his lack of organization and carelessness about money; and that of the two men, only Einstein might be commonly described as eccentric.

For neuroticism, both would probably score low ('emotionally stable', not 'prone to stress and worry'). Neither suffered from depression or fits of temper, and neither was by nature a worrier, or he would not have survived as an independent creative figure, especially Mozart, who lacked the security of being a court composer. Both had overwhelming confidence in their talents, which enabled them to take on challenges that would have daunted a less confident person. Nevertheless, Einstein noted of his research on general relativity:

> The years of anxious searching in the dark, with their intense longing, their alternations of confidence and exhaustion and the final emergence into the light – only those who have experienced it can understand that.

For agreeability, the picture is more mixed. Mozart, beginning life as a biddable child performer anxious to please his patrons, would score relatively high ('trusting, empathetic') – certainly in the jaundiced opinion of his misanthropic father Leopold – except in his uncompromising and bitter dealings with his Salzburg employer Archbishop Colloredo, who unceremoniously sacked him. Einstein, by contrast, would probably score nearer the low end of the scale ('uncooperative, hostile'). Although he was generally courteous, there was a dominant streak of independence and self-absorption that could lead to indifference to, or rejection of, people formerly close to them. It caused the breakdown of Einstein's first marriage, a strained relationship with his two sons, and the near-failure of his second marriage. 'Nothing tragic really gets to him, he is in the happy position of being able to shuffle it off. That is also why he can work so well', Einstein's second wife confided to a woman friend soon after the traumatic death of her elder daughter from her first marriage. Low agreeableness is quite common in exceptionally creative people. 'You have to be ruthless and put yourself and your progress first if you want to get on', is Nettle's summary of the situation concerning agreeableness. He adds Oscar Wilde's comment in *De Profundis*: 'Nothing really at any period of my life was ever of the smallest importance to me compared to Art.'

Einstein would surely have agreed in regard to Science. His conscientious determination to work never softened: he was still making mathematical calculations in hospital the day before he died, in his decades-long quest for a unified field theory of gravity and electromagnetism. So would Curie, who continued to work unprotected with strongly radioactive elements up to her death, despite being acutely aware of how they had damaged her eyes and skin. Darwin called his scientific work his 'sole pleasure in life', and said he was 'never happy except when at work', despite the anxiety and ill-health it seems to have caused him. In the arts, too, geniuses have generally continued to work as long as they could. Mozart was still composing his Requiem (K626) on the evening of his death. Van Gogh continued painting to the day he shot himself. Virginia Woolf took her own life when she discerned that the return of her dreaded mental illness would prevent her from writing.

Darwin's life demonstrates with particular clarity how changeable is the personality of exceptionally creative people, and how greatly personality varies from genius to genius. It is quite difficult to believe that the person who experienced and described the romantic adventures of the *Voyage of the Beagle* in the 1830s is the same person who settled down at Down House in the 1840s and published the distinctly unromantic treatise *On the Origin of Species* in 1859.

Consider this, fairly representative, entry from Darwin's *Voyage* dated May 1835, about his journey through the Andes by horse and mule:

In the evening, Captain FitzRoy and myself were dining with Mr Edwards, an English resident well known for his hospitality by all who have visited Coquimbo, when a sharp earthquake happened. I heard the forecoming rumble, but from the screams of the ladies, the running of servants, and the rush of several of the gentlemen to the doorway, I could not distinguish the motion. Some of the women afterwards were crying with terror, and one person said he should not be able to sleep all night, or if he did, it would only be to dream of falling houses. The father of this gentleman had lately lost all his property at Talcuhano, and he himself had only just escaped a falling roof at Valparaiso, in 1822. He mentioned a curious coincidence which then happened: he was playing at cards, when a German, one of the party, got up, and said he would never sit in a room in these countries with the door shut, since, owing to his having done so, he had nearly lost his life at Copiapó. Accordingly he opened the door, and no sooner had he done this, than he cried out, 'Here it comes again!' and the famous shock commenced. The whole party escaped. The danger in an earthquake is not from the time lost in opening a door, but from the chance of its becoming jammed by the movement of the walls.

Less than ten years later, at Down House, such a tumultuously social evening had become unthinkable for Darwin. In the 1840s,

10. Portrait of Charles Darwin by George Richmond, 1840, around the time that Darwin discovered the principle of natural selection

he developed a clockwork routine revolving around long hours of solitary work in his study – which was banned to his family – and in his garden, interrupted by meals, light reading, a long and unaccompanied walk, and scheduled visitors, with occasional trips to London and a few other places in Britain. Admittedly, this routine was partly to control his chronic ill-health, which started around 1840, but it was also a deliberate policy, so as to reserve the maximum time for research. On the *Beagle* voyage, Darwin had willingly laid himself open to as many new encounters and experiences – scientific, anthropological, and simply human – as chanced to come his way. At Down House, by contrast, his creativity flourished in an atmosphere of *lack* of openness to experience. In due course, he became something of a hermit. Of course, Darwin remained open to the research and opinions of other scientists through his wide reading and vast network of correspondence, but he consciously avoided the variety of accidental encounters and associations typical of his university and globetrotting days.

There was also a change in his neuroticism. The youthful Darwin strikes the reader as rather phlegmatic, with few worries or outbursts of emotion. (Hence, probably, his father's mortifying accusation: 'You care for nothing but shooting, dogs, and rat-catching, and you will be a disgrace to yourself and all your family.') In mid-life, however, Darwin became extremely anxious, even about something as mundane as catching a train to London. The illness of his children, two of whom died prematurely, was one easily understandable cause. So was money – less understandably, given his handsome private income. His overriding anxiety, though, concerned his evolutionary theory and its potentially scandalous public reception, a neurosis that apparently brought on his own desperate and untreatable illness. That is why he wrote out the theory in 1844 and gave the essay to his wife Emma with instructions for its publication in the event of his early death. Thereafter, until 1859, it was his neuroticism that drove his dogged research programme to bolster the scientific evidence for the controversial theory.

Overall, it is plain that there is neither a specific configuration of traits nor are there specific proportions of traits – no 'creative personality', in other words – that underlie exceptional creativity. All geniuses share a personality that is highly motivated to work and determined to succeed in their field. However, the source of this motivation and determination cannot be analysed according to any simple model. Some degree of extraversion, neuroticism, conscientiousness, agreeableness, and openness is required for genius, along with other factors, like intellectual ability and talent. But the interaction of all these factors seems to be more complex, variable, and sensitive to context in geniuses than among ordinary people.

# Chapter 7
# Arts versus sciences

If we set aside the tiny handful of geniuses such as Leonardo and Wren, who were almost equally versed in art and science, it is fair to say that there is virtually no artist who deserves an entry in the scientific reference books, and scarcely any scientist who has made a major contribution to the arts. Perhaps Goethe might qualify in the first category for his 1810 theory of colours, and Freud in the second category for his 1899 theory of dreams and the unconscious, although both theories remain controversial. (Moreover, was Freud really a scientist?) So might the physicist Thomas Young's kick-start to the decipherment of the Rosetta Stone and the Egyptian hieroglyphs around 1815. Arthur C. Clarke might also be a contender for his publication of the concept of the communications satellite in the technical magazine *Wireless World* in 1945, before he abandoned active physics and engineering to became a science-fiction writer. And then there is the captivating example of Tom Lehrer, a Harvard University mathematics lecturer who became one of the most quoted satirical songwriters of the 20th century, although it must be admitted that he does not qualify as a major mathematician.

Lehrer certainly saw a connection between his mathematical training and his musical composition. 'To begin a song is not hard, it's where you are going to end that's hard. You gotta have the joke at the end', he said in an interview in 2000.

> The logical mind, the precision, is the same that's involved in math as in lyrics. And I guess in music too…It's like a puzzle, to write a song. The idea of fitting all the pieces so it exactly comes right, the right word at the end of the sentence, and the rhyme goes there and not there.

Mathematicians, unlike natural scientists, are enthralled by elegance, Lehrer stressed.

> That's the word you hear in mathematics all the time. 'This proof is elegant!' It doesn't really matter what it proves. 'Look at this – isn't that amazing!' And it comes out at the end. It's neat. It's not just that it's proof, because there are plenty of proofs that are just boring proofs. But every now and then there's a really elegant proof.

Lehrer gave an example from his own song-writing, after citing a comment on rhyme from the autobiography of the mathematician Stanislaw Ulam (who helped to build the atomic bomb) that rhyming 'forces novel associations…and becomes a sort of automatic mechanism of originality'. In Lehrer's classic song 'Wernher von Braun', about the amoral German rocket engineer who first built the V2 rocket for the Nazis and then the Saturn V rockets for the US Apollo programme, there are the rhymed lines: '"Once the rocket goes up who cares where it comes down?/ That's not my department", says Wernher von Braun.' According to Lehrer: 'If "Von Braun" didn't happen to rhyme with "down" (and a few other words), the most quoted couplet in the song would not exist, and in all probability the song itself would not have been written.'

Lehrer's argument seems to imply that there is more in common between mathematical discovery and artistic creation than meets the eye. Numbers follow rules – of addition, multiplication, commutation, and so on – which generate mathematics; and so do words, if they are to make meaningful prose and poetry. But of course, there is a crucial difference between mathematical and linguistic rules: mathematical rules are natural and eternally valid, whereas the rules of grammar, syntax, and pronunciation for any spoken language are invented and change over time. Mathematical truth exists independently of humankind, so we think, whereas linguistic meaning has no existence beyond that of human beings. 'Our natural point of view in regard to the existence of truth apart from humanity cannot be explained or proved, but it is a belief which nobody can lack – not even primitive beings', Einstein told Tagore (who disagreed) in a conversation in 1930. 'We attribute to truth a superhuman objectivity. It is indispensable for us – this reality which is independent of our existence and our experience and our mind – though we cannot say what it means.'

This is why we generally speak of 'discovering' a mathematical or a scientific truth, yet 'creating' a work of art. The principle of natural selection was discovered by Darwin in the 1830s, yet it had existed in nature since the beginning of life on earth and could have been discovered by someone else; in fact it was independently discovered by Alfred Russel Wallace in 1858, which forced Darwin to publish his theory or lose his priority. The theory of special relativity was almost discovered by the mathematician Henri Poincaré around 1900, not Einstein. The structure of DNA was nearly discovered by Linus Pauling, and also Rosalind Franklin, rather than by Crick and Watson. 'In science, what X misses today Y will surely hit upon tomorrow (or maybe the day after tomorrow). Much of a scientist's pride and sense of accomplishment turns therefore upon being the *first* to do something,' wrote the Nobel laureate Peter Medawar in 1964, encapsulating a view widely shared by scientists. 'Artists are not troubled by matters of priority, but Wagner would certainly not have spent 20 years on *The Ring* if he had thought it at all possible for someone else to nip in ahead of him with *Götterdämmerung*.'

In science and technology, unlike the arts, multiple independent discovery of the same idea or phenomenon appears to be quite common. Instances, with approximate dates, include: the discovery of sunspots by Galileo in 1610, and by three other individuals independently in 1611; the discovery of the calculus by Newton in 1671, and by Leibniz in 1676; the invention of photography by Louis Daguerre, and by William Henry Fox Talbot, in 1839; the discovery of ether anaesthesia in surgery by Crawford Long in 1842, and by William Morton in 1846; the discovery of the conservation of energy by Julius Robert Mayer in 1843, by Hermann Helmholtz in 1847, and by James Joule in 1847; the discovery of evolution by natural selection by Darwin in 1838, and by Wallace in 1858; the discovery of the periodic table of the chemical elements by Béguyer de Chancourtois in 1862, by John Newlands in 1864, by Julius Lothar Meyer in 1864, and by Dmitri Mendeleev in 1869; the invention of the telephone by Alexander Graham Bell, and by Elisha Gray, in 1876; the invention of the incandescent carbon-filament lamp by Edison, and by Joseph Swan, in 1878; and the discovery of insulin in 1921 by Frederick Banting and Charles Best, and by Nicolas Paulesco around 1921. Multiple discoveries and inventions became much rarer in the 20th century, as scientific communication became faster. As soon as the structure of DNA was published in 1953, for example, other investigators working on the problem, such as Pauling, abandoned their efforts.

In 1979, Simonton investigated and analysed multiple discoveries in detail. He found the overwhelming majority of cases to be doublets, that is, two claimants to be the discoverer. There were 449 doublets, 104 triplets, 18 quadruplets, 7 quintuplets, and 1 octuplet. On the face of it, such a list is good evidence for Medawar's theory of science and the arts. Ideas and phenomena exist 'out there' in Einstein's objective reality, waiting to be discovered by any scientist who is intelligent enough, whereas art comes from inside the mind, created by the unique desires of the individual artist. However, the evidence looks weaker when carefully examined.

For a start, over three-quarters of the multiple discoveries are doublets: 449 out of 579. If the Medawar theory is correct, we should surely expect a higher proportion of triplets, quadruplets, and higher-grade multiples. Secondly, many of the multiples are not strictly simultaneous, despite being independent. Only about one-fifth of them took place within a one-year interval. The wider the spread in the dates of the multiple discoveries, the less they support the theory, because they may not be as independent as they seem. Five years elapsed between Newton's and Leibniz's discovery of the calculus (which led Newton to accuse Leibniz of plagiarism). There was a gap of some 20 years, almost a generation, between Darwin's and Wallace's discoveries of natural selection, and an even longer gap, 35 years, between Gregor Mendel's discovery of genetic laws in 1865 and their co-discovery in 1900 by Hugo de Vries, Carl Correns, and Erich von Tschermak, each of whom worked independently. Lastly, what appears to be a multiple may in fact not be a case of true identity, thereby casting doubt on the whole claim that frequent multiple discoveries occur. In a doublet, the 'same' discoveries may have only one or two elements in common out of many elements; moreover, the two processes of arriving at the same discovery may be quite different. Nobel prizes for a single discovery in science are very often shared between three scientists, each of whom has looked at the same problem from a different perspective and contributed differently to the discovery – as happened with the structure of DNA, where the Nobel prize was shared between Crick, Watson, and Maurice Wilkins in 1962. When nuclear magnetic resonance was discovered in 1946 by two groups of American scientists working independently of each other, one at Harvard University and the other at Stanford University, to begin with one group was literally unable to understand what the other group was talking about, because their two approaches to the physical phenomenon they had discovered differed so radically.

Thus, the distinction between scientific discovery and artistic creation tends to disappear on closer examination to some extent. Scientific breakthroughs are not simply waiting to happen; they occur in a historical context. Artistic breakthroughs are not born virginally; they have antecedents in other work. Both scientific discoveries and artistic creations require a combination of individual and consensual thinking. Earlier thinkers on evolution influenced Darwin; the same is true in physics of Einstein's work on relativity and quantum theory; previous Renaissance paintings of 'The Last Supper' influenced Leonardo's painting; contemporary Italian operas influenced Mozart's *The Marriage of Figaro*; and so on. This has led some psychologists to see artistic and scientific creativity as being located on a theoretical continuum, rather than in separate compartments. Weisberg, for instance, visualizes at the left-hand extreme of the continuum God's creation of something out of nothing and at the right-hand extreme a person's discovery of a dollar bill in the street. Artistic creativity then occupies the left-hand side and centre of the continuum, where it overlaps with scientific creativity, which occupies the centre and right-hand side of the continuum. 'From this perspective,' writes Weisberg, 'it is not absurd to say that Watson and Crick created the double helix, although it seems less acceptable to say that Picasso discovered *Guernica*.'

The point has been forcefully argued by the molecular biologist and philosopher of science Gunther Stent over many years, beginning with the publication of Watson's memoir *The Double Helix* in 1968, a book that took essentially the same line on scientific discovery as Medawar. Stent argues that:

> the structure of the DNA molecule was not what it was before Watson and Crick defined it, because there was and there still is no such thing as the DNA molecule in the natural world. The DNA molecule is an abstraction created by century-long efforts of a succession of biochemists, all of whom selected for their attention certain ensembles of natural phenomena. The DNA double helix is as much a creation as it is a discovery...

In Stent's view, 'as applied to art and science, the antinomy of discovery versus creation has little philosophical merit'.

He has a good point. DNA is often said – even by commentators who should know better – to have been 'discovered' by Watson and Crick. In fact, it was discovered in 1869; its role in genetic inheritance was discovered in 1943; and its double-helix structure was discovered in 1953. Thus, the scientific conception of DNA changed radically in this time period, even though DNA's function in nature remained precisely the same.

**11. James Watson and Francis Crick with their model of DNA, the 'double helix', 1953**

But Stent, and Weisberg, are less convincing in arguing for the similarity between the 'creation' of DNA's structure and the creation of a work of art. Weisberg compares the discovery of the structure in 1953 with the painting of *Guernica* by Picasso in 1937, for which Picasso kept detailed and dated sketches. From both these and *The Double Helix*, it is plain that Picasso, and Crick and Watson, were systematic in their approaches, and that the artist and the two scientists were influenced by pre-existing works. But in the DNA case, the influences, such as Pauling's and Franklin's work, are easily identified and their working is clearly understood, whereas Picasso never names his influences, forcing Weisberg to speculate.

He chooses, reasonably enough, a 1935 etching by Picasso, *Minotauromachy*, which shares elements with *Guernica* – most evidently the bull and the raised head of a horse – plus an etching from Francisco de Goya's 19th-century *Disasters of War*, which Picasso definitely admired. In this etching, Weisberg identifies, for example, a mother figure by Goya with a posture (somewhat) similar to that of Picasso's woman with her dead child in *Guernica*, and also claims that Picasso changed a falling man with outstretched hands in Goya's etching into a falling woman in *Guernica*, because: 'Her profile is similar to that of Goya's man, and her outstretched hands with exaggeratedly splayed fingers echo those of the Goya figure.' Maybe, maybe not: Picasso does not tell us. For Weisberg, such resemblances show there to be 'layers of antecedents to *Guernica*' – as with the structure of DNA. Of this there is no doubt, but was Picasso thinking of such antecedents while painting *Guernica*? Even if they were in his conscious mind, it is not the borrowed elements that make a work of art, but, rather obviously, the way that they are transformed by the artist to make a whole. Surely Goya did influence Picasso, but if Picasso really is of Goya's stature, his borrowings from Goya in *Guernica* will have been subtler and more complex than Weisberg's suggested connections. If Weisberg's literal-minded analysis were true of Picasso, it would actually reduce, not enhance, the quality of his painting. Contrary to Weisberg's intention, his comparison suggests that creative science and artistic creation, at the level of genius, are more separate, than similar, activities.

'It is bizarre how very little of 20th-century science has been assimilated into 20th-century art', the scientifically trained novelist C. P. Snow observed in 1959 in *The Two Cultures*. Despite increased efforts at assimilation since then, the results remain meagre. It is a rare artist who can illuminate scientific concepts, the process of scientific discovery, and the working life of scientists. The greatest painters and sculptors have neglected these subjects. The same is true of great film-makers: they leave them to lesser talents, who make movies such as *Madame Curie*, *A Beautiful Mind* (about John Nash), and *Flash of Genius* (about the inventor of the intermittent windscreen-wiper, Robert Kearns), which, though often enjoyable and well acted, invariably concentrate on personalities at the expense of science. Stage productions about science that rely on argument about ideas and ethics have a better chance of artistic success, for example the play *Copenhagen* (on the wartime meeting of Bohr and Heisenberg), as opposed to those that resort to exciting stage effects and intrusive music to distract the audience from the paucity of real science, such as *A Disappearing Number* (about Ramanujan), and operas like *Doctor Atomic* (on Robert Oppenheimer and the Manhattan Project) and *Einstein on the Beach*. Perhaps the best results have been obtained on the page, by fiction writers who began their careers with a scientific training, such as Arthur C. Clarke and Fred Hoyle, rather than novelists who in later life pick up science from their own research, like Martin Amis and Ian McEwan. Even so, the depiction of science in fiction is yet to reach the heights of great literature.

Generally speaking, leading artists are not very interested in science – certainly much less interested than leading scientists are in the arts. Marie Curie enjoyed reading literature in Polish,

French, German, Russian, and English, for example. Einstein was deeply interested in music, especially Bach and Mozart, whose piano and violin works he knew well and sometimes performed in public. He even stated that: 'Mozart's music is so pure and beautiful that I see it as a reflection of the inner beauty of the universe.' But Mozart had virtually no recorded interest in science, apart from his friendship with the controversial physician Anton Mesmer, inventor of mesmerism, which Mozart spoofed in his opera *Così fan tutte*. Among the dozen or so contemporary artists recently interviewed by John Tusa for the BBC (listed in Chapter 3), science barely makes an appearance: only two of the interviewees mention science in passing, and one of them is an architect who is constantly immersed in questions of engineering. Tusa, it is necessary to say, asks no questions about science, yet this cannot entirely explain the silence of the interviewees. None of them makes even a casual reference to Darwin, Einstein, or Freud, let alone any psychologist, in over 250 pages of published interviews. Judging from Tusa's *On Creativity*, artists and scientists appear to inhabit separate worlds.

The notorious division of society into Snow's 'two cultures' – the humanistic and the scientific – which do not communicate, is still alive, if not as clear-cut as it was. The intellectual arrogance once common on both sides may have diminished, but it has not given way to widespread enthusiasm for bridging the gap. In fact, the gap is widening with the increasing specialization of education and science and the escalating sophistication of technology. 'Any sufficiently advanced technology is indistinguishable from magic', Clarke commented half a century ago, as satellites began to be used for global telecommunications. The idea of a 21st-century equivalent of Leonardo or Wren is sadly now a forlorn fantasy.

# Chapter 8
# Eureka experiences

In both the arts and the sciences, genius is sometimes associated with a 'eureka experience': a sudden, surprising illumination that produces a breakthrough. A modern instance is the invention of DNA fingerprinting. The experienced geneticist Alec Jeffreys discovered its underlying concept accidentally, whilst doing an experiment intended to study how inherited illnesses such as cystic fibrosis were passed through families. In order to trace genes through family lineages, Jeffreys had identified a fragment of DNA that repeated on different chromosomes in the cells of men and women. He had then devised a technique, by tagging the DNA fragment with a radioactive molecule, to count these repeated sections on X-ray film in different individuals and their relatives. Having left the experiment running over the weekend, he returned to his laboratory on Monday morning, 10 September 1984, to find a peculiar array of blobs and lines on the developed film. His first reaction was: 'God, what a mess.' But when he stared at the data a bit longer, 'The penny dropped.' Each sequence of bars on the film represented a different number of DNA repeats: a bar code that was unique to an individual and was also a composite of the DNA of the individual's father and mother. 'It was an absolute eureka moment,' Jeffreys said later.

It was a blinding flash. In five golden minutes, my research career went whizzing off in a completely new direction. The last thing that had been on my mind was anything to do with identification or paternity suits. However, I would have been a complete idiot not to spot the applications.

The archetypal eureka experience is of course that of Archimedes. When taking his bath two millennia ago, Archimedes is said to have perceived the principles of displacement and flotation, jumped out of the tub, and run naked through the city streets with a cry of 'Eureka!' – Greek for (roughly speaking) 'I've got it!'. Johannes Gutenberg provides another example from science and technology. Whilst casually watching a wine press during the grape harvest in the 15th century, Gutenberg supposedly got the idea for the printing press. Isaac Newton, seeing an apple fall from a tree in the 17th century, apparently visualized the law of gravitational attraction. Dmitri Mendeleev, whilst writing a chemistry textbook in 1869, is said to have taken a nap and had a dream; on awakening, he wrote down the periodic table of the elements. James Watson, whilst playing with cardboard models of biomolecules in 1953, suddenly saw how the two halves of the structure of DNA fitted together, and thereby solved the essential biomolecular mechanism of heredity. 'My morale skyrocketed', writes Watson in *The Double Helix*.

In the arts, eureka experiences tend not to be so clear-cut, although key ideas come just as suddenly and surprisingly as in the sciences. A. E. Housman described his own creative process in his lectures, *The Name and Nature of Poetry*. 'Having drunk a pint of beer at luncheon', he writes:

> I would go out for a walk of two or three hours. As I went along, thinking of nothing in particular, only looking at things around me and following the progress of the seasons, there would flow into my mind, with sudden and unaccountable emotion, sometimes a line or two of verse, sometimes a whole stanza at once, accompanied, not

preceded, by a vague notion of the poem which they were destined to form part of. Then there would usually be a lull of an hour or so, then perhaps the spring would bubble up again.

More dramatically, like a eureka experience, Coleridge claimed in 1816 that whilst reading a passage in a book about the 'Khan Kubla' in the late 18th century, he fell into an opium-induced sleep, and when he awoke, immediately produced the poem 'Kubla Khan: Or, A Vision in a Dream' ('In Xanadu did Kubla Khan/ A stately pleasure-dome decree...'). Closer in time, in 1932, Henri Cartier-Bresson, chancing in Paris upon a photograph of African boys running, taken by the sports photographer Martin Munkácsi, decided to take up photography in earnest. 'I suddenly understood that photography can fix eternity in a moment. It is the only photo that influenced me', Cartier-Bresson recalled in the 1970s. 'I felt it like a kick up the backside: go on, have a go!' In 1950, Satyajit Ray, during a screening of the recently released Italian film *Bicycle Thieves* in London, immediately grasped how he would make his classic first film *Pather Panchali* back in India. 'It just gored me', Ray wrote in 1982.

The further back in history we go, the slimmer is the evidence for eureka experiences. There is nothing at all in the case of Archimedes, except hearsay; only one rather doubtful letter from Gutenberg; no written statement about the apple from Newton, only remarks made to others in old age; and considerable confusion surrounding Mendeleev's dream, which was reported at second-hand by a colleague. With Coleridge's dream, the long gap between the composition of 'Kubla Khan' in 1797 and its publication in 1816 creates doubt about the authenticity of the poet's account of its composition. The scholar Elisabeth Schneider examined all of the surviving evidence in Coleridge's manuscripts and letters and came to the conclusion that 'Kubla Khan' was composed in a much more conventional manner, not in a dream but in various highly conscious drafts. A second Coleridge scholar, Richard Holmes, whilst not discounting the dream altogether, noted: 'it is difficult to accept that the chanting, hypnotic, high finished language of "Kubla Khan" is *literally* as Coleridge dreamt it'.

Yet, such anecdotes cannot be discounted as simply false, because there are numerous reliable accounts of flashes of inspiration by both scientists and artists. Moreover, they chime with our personal experience: we all know that good ideas can spring unheralded from casual conversations, chance associations, leaps of imagination, and irrational inputs such as dreams.

On the other hand, eureka experiences are by no means the whole story. A great idea may have seemed to arrive 'out of the blue', but before this the mind seems to have prepared itself by long study. The individuals concerned were long immersed in thinking about problems in the field of their eventual breakthrough. Jeffreys and DNA fingerprinting illustrates this. Alexander Fleming, who discovered penicillin, had been working in the bacteriology department of a London hospital for some two decades before he stumbled upon the bacteria-killing mould *Penicillium* in 1928. During the First World War, Fleming became interested in finding antibiotics to treat sepsis in the wounds of servicemen. After the war, he began an active programme of research; in 1922, he discovered the antibiotic enzyme lysozyme in nasal mucus, tears, and saliva. Fleming's discovery of penicillin is a textbook example of Louis Pasteur's dictum: 'Where observation is concerned, chance favours only the prepared mind.'

Let us put under the microscope, as it were, one of the most celebrated scientific eureka experiences: the discovery of the hexagonal ring structure of six carbon atoms in the benzene molecule by the German chemist August Kekulé in the 1860s. This was a crucial step in the foundation of organic chemistry. It offers an excellent illustration of the complexity of real eureka experiences.

**12. August Kekulé on a postage stamp of the German Democratic Republic, 1979. It shows the hexagonal carbon ring of benzene that the chemist claimed to have first visualized in a dream**

In 1890, a quarter of a century after the event, Kekulé recollected what happened in a public speech. A first flash of inspiration occurred some time in 1855 while he was riding home on top of a London omnibus in a 'reverie' on a summer's evening after talking chemistry with a friend. Before the conductor at last cried out 'Clapham Road', Kekulé had visualized a dance of atoms, large and small, forming pairs, threesomes, and combinations up to a valency of four, making chains of atoms. But the breakthrough came about seven years later while dozing in front of a fire, he said:

> During my residence in Ghent, in Belgium, I lived in an elegant bachelor apartment on the main street. However, my study was situated along a narrow alley and had no light during the day. For a chemist who spends his day in the laboratory this was not a disadvantage. [One evening] I was sitting there, working on my textbook, but it was not going well; my thoughts were on other matters. I turned my chair towards the fireplace and sank into

half-sleep. Again the atoms fluttered before my eyes. This time smaller groups remained modestly in the background. My mental eye, sharpened by repeated visions of a similar kind, now distinguished larger forms in a variety of combinations. Long chains, often combined in a denser fashion; everything in motion, twisting and turning like snakes. But look, what was that?! One of the snakes had seized its own tail, and the figure whirled mockingly before my eyes. I awoke in a flash, and this time, too, I spent the rest of the night working out the consequences of the hypothesis.

Kekulé concluded:

Gentlemen, let us learn to dream, and perhaps then we will find the truth…but let us also beware not to publish our dreams until they have been examined by the wakened mind.

It is a compelling picture: the most famous dream in the history of science. Perhaps too compelling to be strictly true. Indeed, some historians of chemistry have doubted if any such day-dream occurred. However, there is evidence that Kekulé told the story to family and friends many times during his life before finally publishing it in 1890: this is what his son testified; and in 1886, a well-known spoof inspired by the dream snakes seizing their own tails was published, which suggests that the story had already circulated widely. Furthermore, Kekulé was known for his caution as a chemist, unlike some of his contemporaries, so it is not likely that he would publicize a bizarre dream if it were not basically true. Assuming it did happen, how much weight can be placed on it as describing a eureka experience?

In 1858, well before the breakthrough, Kekulé had published a paper setting out his structural theory of how four-valent carbon atoms become linked to form open-chain ('aliphatic') molecules, followed by the first volume of his textbook in 1859–61; but during this time he made no published mention of the structure of closed-chain ('aromatic') molecules such as benzene, bar one very cryptic reference that shows he was thinking about the problem. The dream appears to have taken place early in 1862, or at least before Kekulé got married in June of that year (since he refers in his speech to his 'bachelor apartment'). He did not actually publish his closed-chain ring structure of benzene until 1865–6, some three years after the dream.

This period, the late 1850s and early 1860s, was one of spectacular growth in the coal-tar dye industry and also the petroleum industry. Knowledge of organic chemistry expanded rapidly in chemical laboratories, and some of the newly discovered aromatic compounds were clearly similar to benzene (which had been discovered in compressed oil-gas in 1825 by Faraday). But what was lacking was a concomitant theory of chemical structure into which the new knowledge could be fitted. Several chemists other than Kekulé were trying to work out the molecular structure of benzene. Josef Loschmidt, for instance, proposed three alternative benzene formulae in 1861, none involving a ring structure; however Loschmidt chose to symbolize benzene with a large circle to indicate that it was still structurally indeterminate. Archibald Couper hypothesized ring structures in 1858 for two different organic compounds, but neither of them was benzene. Kekulé was not at all convinced by their work, yet revealed little about his reasons, either in print or in correspondence. It appears that he deliberately kept his thoughts on the subject to himself, while remaining fully abreast of competing ideas. Presumably, though, the speculations of Loschmidt, Couper, and other chemists were among the many ideas jostling in Kekulé's mind as he attempted to write a further volume of his organic chemistry textbook and, one evening in 1862, fell into a doze by the fire.

His delay in publishing his theory was partly for personal reasons. His wife died in childbirth in 1863, leaving him with an infant son and a feeling of depression and lack of purpose. But he was also waiting for experimental evidence of the existence of novel compounds predictable on the basis of a ring structure for benzene. This appeared only in 1864, in the work of two chemists who synthesized ethyl- and amyl-phenyl, benzene-related compounds with structures and properties Kekulé expected on the basis of his as-yet-unpublished theory. These new experimental results pushed him into action and triggered the publication of his theory in January 1865.

Confusingly, his breakthrough paper began by claiming that his closed-chain theory was 'fully formed' in 1858 – that is, long before the dream in his apartment in Ghent – moreover, the paper failed to emphasize either the benzene ring structure or its potential derivative structures. Nevertheless, the benzene ring was undeniably stated. The more Kekulé now thought about it, the more his theory of aromatics seemed elegant: 'an inexhaustible treasure-trove', as he told a student in April 1865. Within months, he and his students, working in the laboratory, were able to report the synthesis of further novel compounds (polybromo- and polyiodobenzenes) explained by the ring structure of the benzene nucleus. In 1866, he published three-dimensional perspective drawings of benzene. The ring was quickly accepted in principle by almost all organic chemists, because its theoretical predictions received such extensive experimental confirmation.

Kekulé's dream was therefore part of a continuous period of enquiry into the structure of benzene over more than five years up to 1865, not an isolated insight. It was not truly the eureka experience he implied (he did not use the actual word eureka) – emotionally important though the dream clearly was to Kekulé. Most probably, he started contemplating a ring structure in the late 1850s well before his dream; persuaded his 'wakened mind' of its existence from 1862 onwards; but felt insufficiently confident to go public until after the publication of experimental support by others in 1864. 'Contrary to most accounts, and to the implication of the dream anecdote told out of context, it is now clear that the benzene theory did not fall into Kekulé's half-awake mind fully formed – or even partially formed', writes Alan J. Rocke, after exhaustive consideration of the historical evidence.

> It was at most the ring *concept* that arrived by this semi-conscious or unconscious process, a concept which…was not without precedent. The theory itself was developed only slowly, one might even say painfully, over the course of several years, before its first codification in 1866.

Such gradual evolution turns out to be typical of creative breakthroughs, when their histories are examined in detail. They may or may not involve a recognizable eureka experience, but they are always preceded by a long period of thought and labour, and always followed by intensive scrutiny and development. Here are two more examples – the first of them from the ancient world, the second from the late 20th century.

The anonymous invention of writing might be said to be the ur-breakthrough, since there would be no history, no science, and no literature (other than oral traditions) without it. How did so momentous an invention occur? 'Proto-writing' – that is, signs capable of expressing a limited range of meaning but not the full range of spoken language – seems to have existed during the last Ice Age, in the form of enigmatic cave drawings, petroglyphs, and notched bones, perhaps 20,000 years old. (Modern examples of 'proto-writing' include international transportation symbols at airports, mathematical symbols, and musical staff notation.) 'Full writing' – that is, a sign system able to express any and all thought – most likely started some five millennia ago in the expanding cities of Mesopotamia, in the form of pictographic and other symbols that fairly quickly evolved into wedge-shaped cuneiform marks inscribed in clay tablets. The Egyptian hieroglyphs appeared very soon after the earliest cuneiform, around 3000 BC, perhaps under the influence of neighbouring Mesopotamia, although this link is unproven.

The breakthrough that transformed proto-writing into full writing was the *rebus*. The word comes from a Latin word meaning 'by things'. Rebuses permit spoken words to be written in terms of their constituent parts – vowels, consonants, syllables, and so on – that cannot be depicted pictographically. With the rebus principle, the sounds of a language can be made visible in a systematic way, and its abstract concepts symbolized. Rebus writing is familiar today from puzzle-picture writing, and also to some extent from electronic text messaging. An English rebus would be a picture of a bee with a picture of a tray standing for 'betray', or the symbols 'b4' standing for 'before' in a text message. In Egyptian hieroglyphs, which are full of rebuses, the 'sun' pictogram (a dot in a circle), pronounced *r(a)* or *r(e)*, stands for the sun god Ra and is also the first symbol in the hieroglyphic spelling of the pharaoh known to us as Ramesses the Great.

How was the rebus conceived? Some scholars believe it resulted from a conscious search by an unknown Sumerian 'genius' in Uruk (biblical Erech), c. 3300 BC – the place and date of the earliest clay tablets that apparently record full writing. Others posit invention by a group, presumably of clever administrators and merchants. Still others think it was an accidental discovery, not an invention. Many regard it as the result of lengthy evolution from proto-writing, not of a eureka experience by an individual inventor. These are all reasonable hypotheses, given the severely limited evidence, and we shall probably never know which is actually correct.

What is certain, from the archaeological evidence, is that proto-writing existed long before full writing; and that cuneiform took centuries to develop the capacity to record advanced thought such as poetry. The world's oldest surviving literature, in Sumerian cuneiform, dates from about 2600 BC, although these early tablets remain extremely difficult to read, because the script did not yet express language fully. In other words, there must once, in the late fourth millennium BC, have been a breakthrough into rebus writing – yet to modern eyes writing appears to have been a gradual development during the third millennium, without any eureka moment.

Moving forward five millennia, the World Wide Web launched in 1990–1 took about ten years to invent, beginning with an experimental web-like computer programme, known as Enquire, written by Tim Berners-Lee in 1980 as a sort of 'intranet' for physicists working at CERN, the European Laboratory for Particle Physics. In 1999, Berners-Lee recalled: 'The Web resulted from many influences on my mind, half-formed thoughts, disparate conversations, and seemingly disconnected experiments.' He deliberately eschews the word 'eureka'. 'Journalists have always asked me what the crucial idea was, or what the singular event was, that allowed the Web to exist one day when it hadn't the day before. They are frustrated when I tell them there was no "eureka" moment', writes Berners-Lee in his memoir *Weaving the Web*.

Even so, many breakthroughs do seem to have involved a eureka experience. (Another term might be 'epiphany', which is favoured by the Nobel prize-winning physicist Leon Lederman.) One certainly occurred in Newton's discovery of gravity in 1665–6, in Champollion's decipherment of the Egyptian hieroglyphs in September 1822, in Darwin's discovery of natural selection in September 1838, in Einstein's discovery of special relativity in May 1905, and in Watson's discovery of the biomolecular mechanism of heredity in February 1953. Whatever name one chooses to give it, an identifiable episode of sudden insight following a long period of intensive study was experienced by each of these geniuses.

# Chapter 9
# **Perspiration and inspiration**

Gradual preparation with sudden illumination, dogged work with a eureka experience, perspiration with inspiration – whichever way we choose to put it – are defining features of genius. 'Before the gates of Excellence the high gods have placed sweat', said an unnamed ancient Greek poet who predated Plato (probably Hesiod). In Edison's much-quoted words, dating from around 1903, 'Genius is one per cent inspiration, ninety-nine per cent perspiration.' Another version of this idea, attributed to George Bernard Shaw, alters the proportions to 'ninety per cent perspiration, ten per cent inspiration'. Late in life, Darwin made the same basic point less pithily but with profound insight in a letter to his son Horace, as follows:

> I have been speculating last night what makes a man a discoverer of undiscovered things, and a most perplexing problem it is. – Many men who are very clever, – much cleverer than the discoverers – never originate anything. As far as I can conjecture, the art consists in habitually searching for causes or meaning of everything which occurs. This implies sharp observation and requires as much knowledge as possible of the subject investigated.

There can be no doubting that, like Darwin, geniuses work habitually and continually. Edison was the owner of 1093 patents, lodging an average of one patent every two weeks of his adult life; J. S. Bach on average composed 20 pages of finished music per day – sufficient to keep a copyist occupied for a lifetime of standard working hours in writing out the parts by hand; Picasso created more than 20,000 works; Henri Poincaré published 500 papers and 30 books; Einstein produced 240 publications; Freud had 330. 'These figures lead one to realize a very important fact – these people must have spent the major

**13. Thomas Edison with his original dynamo, *c.* 1906, not long after he remarked: 'Genius is one per cent inspiration, ninety-nine per cent perspiration.'**

part of their waking hours and their energy on their work', comments Ochse in *Before the Gates of Excellence: The Determinants of Creative Genius*.

Geniuses tend to be prolific, compared with their contemporaries, and to continue producing up to their dying days, as was the case with Einstein and Mozart. The indefatigable Thomas Young worked on the proofs of his *Rudiments of an Egyptian Dictionary* when he lay dying in 1829 in his mid-fifties, able to manage only a pencil instead of his customary pen. As a professional physician, Young had a better idea of his medical condition than most patients have. But when a close friend remonstrated with him that the writing would exhaust him, Young answered:

> that it was a work which if he should live it would be a satisfaction
> to him to have finished, but that if it were otherwise, which seemed
> most probable, as he had never witnessed a complaint which
> appeared to make more rapid progress, it would still be a great
> satisfaction to him never to have spent an idle day in his life.

However, there is little consensus among creators – geniuses or otherwise – as to whether or not perspiration is separate from inspiration. 'This whole business of creation, of the ideas that come in a flash, cannot be explained by science. It cannot. I don't know what can explain it but I know that the best ideas come at moments when you're not even thinking of it. It's a very private thing really,' Satyajit Ray maintained. Inspiration evidently arises, 'unbidden and incomprehensible to its very begetter' (writes psychologist Chris McManus), from both concentrated work on a problem and from apparently unrelated work. Most likely, inspiration and perspiration are inseparable twins. 'If there is inspiration, it's not something that comes at the beginning of the piece. It comes in the course of writing it,' the composer Elliott Carter remarked. 'The more I get into the piece the more the inspiration – well, I don't know exactly what inspiration means – but I would see more clearly and with more excitement and more interest new things, and would not be in the process of discarding a great many things I don't want to do.' On the other hand, a second composer, Aaron Copland, said:

> You can't pick the moment when you are going to have ideas. It picks you and then you might be completely absorbed in another piece of work...I think composers will tell you that they get ideas when they can't possibly work on them. They put them down where they can find them when they need to look for ideas and they don't come easily.

As for where an idea comes from, the possibilities seem to be as diverse as the individual creators. The sculptor Anthony Caro said of himself:

> There are so many ways in which it comes. It comes from thinking about art. It comes from looking at art. It comes from a conversation you had. It comes from the last work you did. It comes from what the architects are doing. It comes from paintings you saw. It comes from seeing two bits of steel on the ground together or it comes from coming across something and saying, 'That's a start, now wait a minute, what else does it need?'

Over the past century, many psychologists, such as Graham Wallas, Arthur Koestler, Mihalyi Csikszentmihalyi, David Perkins, Dean Keith Simonton, Robert Sternberg, and Robert Weisberg attempted to design theories of creativity. None of these was truly explanatory, which is why this book has neglected them thus far. But it is worthwhile to consider how they failed, by focusing on two of the more prominent theories: those of Csikszentmihalyi and of the economist David Galenson.

In Csikszentmihalyi's domain/field/person model of creativity, creativity is not inherent in a person but emerges from the interaction of a person's work in a domain (for instance, music) with a field of experts (composers and critics). Rather than asking the question, What is creativity?, we should instead ask, *Where* is creativity?, suggests Csikszentmihalyi. The point about experts may seem obvious, yet it contradicts our cherished belief that creativity and genius may be present in individuals, even perhaps in ourselves – yet go unrecognized. Csikszentmihalyi pinpoints this contradiction:

> The usual way to think about this issue is that someone like Van Gogh was a great creative genius, but his contemporaries did not recognize this. Fortunately, now we have discovered what a great painter he was after all, so his creativity has been vindicated. What we are saying is that we know what great art is so much better than Van Gogh's contemporaries did – those bourgeois philistines. What – besides unconscious conceit – warrants this belief? A more objective description of Van Gogh's contribution is that his creativity came into being when a sufficient number of experts felt that his paintings had something important to contribute to the domain of art. Without such a response, Van Gogh would have remained what he was, a disturbed man who painted strange canvases.

Furthermore, according to Csikszentmihalyi's model, a person cannot be creative in a domain if he or she has not been exposed to the domain – either by formal training or by self-education (as with Van Gogh). Moreover, creativity can manifest itself only in domains that already exist.

His model has some merits, not least in acting as a corrective to the common debasement of the word creativity to mean any imaginative expression by an individual, but it is too rigid to encompass genius. How can the model account for, say, Faraday's seminal contributions to physics with only a little knowledge of mathematics, or the poet Tagore's becoming India's leading modernist painter, or the architect Ventris's decipherment of Linear B? Faraday and Tagore lacked the necessary formal training in the domains of mathematics and painting; Ventris operated in a non-existent domain. (There are still no university departments of decipherment.) Anyone who crosses established disciplinary boundaries, manages to make a breakthrough, and forges a new domain – as Darwin did in drawing upon biology, palaeontology, geology, and economics to create his theory of evolution by natural selection – is apparently disqualified from being considered creative by Csikszentmihalyi's model.

A more valuable aspect of the model is its prediction that the appellation 'genius' should come and go with the fluctuating opinions of experts. In other words, geniuses can be made and unmade over long periods; all attributions of genius are provisional. This chimes with the evidence from studies of reputation. In Chapter 1, we saw that J. S. Bach has generally ranked first among musical geniuses in recent decades, though somewhat lower in the first half of the 20th century, when Beethoven was widely considered the greatest composer. But this was far from being true during the second half of the 18th century, when Bach's music was neglected after his death in 1750, except by a few composers, notably Mozart, Haydn, and Beethoven. The change in Bach's reputation began after 1800 and took off in 1829, the centenary of Bach's *St Matthew Passion*, thanks to the 20-year-old composer Felix Mendelssohn's conducting the first performance of the great choral work since Bach's death, at a concert in Berlin. The Bach revival that followed during the 19th and 20th centuries was the first prominent example of the deliberate exhumation of old music, accompanied by biographical and critical studies; and it has subsequently inspired scholarly revivals of other composers. Bach's new status as a 'genius' was clearly the product of expert reappraisal.

Galenson's theory of creativity, as befits an economist, has its origins in the prices paid for paintings made by well-known artists, which he takes to indicate an artist's creative status. In *Old Masters and Young Geniuses*, Galenson notes that the art auction market values Picasso's work most highly when the artist was in his twenties; the prices peak around the time Picasso painted *Les Demoiselles d'Avignon* in 1907, aged 26. With Paul Cézanne, the opposite is true: the market values Cézanne's late work most highly when he was in his sixties. A Picasso work done at the age of 67 sells for less than one-quarter of the price of one done at the age of 26; a Cézanne work painted at the age of 67 is approximately 15 times more expensive than one of the same size painted at the age of 26. A similar pattern is seen in the two artistically distinct generations of American painters who came of age in the decades after the Second World War. The peak prices for works by the abstract expressionists Mark Rothko, Arshile Gorky, Willem de Kooning, Barnett Newman, and Jackson Pollock correspond with the later years of their careers, whereas those for works by the conceptual artists Roy Lichtenstein, Robert Rauschenberg, Andy Warhol, Jasper Johns, and Frank Stella correspond with their early years. Hence the title of Galenson's book: he dubs Cézanne (and Rothko) an 'old master' who matured late, Picasso (and Lichtenstein) a 'young genius' who did his best work early on.

From these facts, Galenson concludes that there have been two very different types of artist in the modern era – not only among painters, but also among poets, novelists, and film directors. The first type, epitomized by Picasso, T. S. Eliot, James Joyce, and Orson Welles, Galenson dubs 'conceptual'; the second, epitomized by Cézanne, Robert Frost, Virginia Woolf, and John Ford, 'experimental'. Essentially, conceptual artists are supposed to find their ideas in their imaginations, plan their works carefully with preparatory sketches, execute them swiftly, and sign them promptly (like Picasso) – whereas experimental artists are supposed to work from external reality without preparatory sketches, seek their material in the process of working, take a long time to create their works, and sometimes fail to sign them (like Cézanne). Because of these two different attitudes to creation, conceptual artists tend to innovate brilliantly whilst young, but later run out of inspiration and repeat themselves – whereas experimental artists break less obviously with tradition when they start out, but through long persistence go on developing with age.

The theory is seductive, however the truth is more prosaic. For example, the most frequently reproduced paintings of Leonardo, Michelangelo, Rembrandt, Titian, Velázquez, and Frans Hals, were created when they were aged 46, 37, 26/36, 36/38, 57, and 79/84, respectively, according to Galenson's research. Yet, despite this wide spread in age, he tries to argue that all six painters should be called experimental artists (in contrast to supposedly conceptual artists like Raphael and Vermeer). He also assigns Van Gogh to the conceptual category, on the grounds that Van Gogh created preparatory sketches, despite the fact that his best work dates from his last two years, not his early years. The even more salient fact that Van Gogh consistently worked from nature, not his imagination (unlike his contemporary Gauguin) – which is proved beyond question by his letters – is simply ignored by Galenson. In reality, it would be more accurate to say that Van Gogh was a fundamentally experimental artist with some conceptual inclinations – like very many other artists. As Galenson is eventually forced by his evidence to admit: 'the two categories I have described in fact stand for a continuous range of variation in practice'.

The only widely respected 'law' of creativity is really the so-called 'ten-year rule'. First identified by John Hayes in 1989 and soon endorsed by several other psychologists, such as Howard Gardner, it states that a person must persevere with learning and practising a craft or discipline for about ten years before he or she can make a breakthrough. Remarkably few breakthroughs have been achieved in less than this time.

The initial scientific evidence for the ten-year rule came from studies in the 1960s and 1970s of chess-players, who take ten years and more to become masters of the game. Then it was found to apply to athletes such as Olympic swimmers, and performers such as concert pianists. Subsequent studies of scientists and mathematicians, composers, painters, and poets – living and deceased – further supported the rule. No rule of human psychology has the universal validity and precision of the laws of physics and chemistry, and this one certainly has some noteworthy exceptions. Yet there are a sufficient number of breakthroughs by scientists and artists that obey the ten-year rule to make it worth taking seriously.

In the sciences, Einstein is a good example. His first insight into the basis of special relativity occurred around 1895, and his theory was created and published in 1905. So is Darwin, whose theory of natural selection was conceived in 1838, ten years after Darwin immersed himself in science at Cambridge University in 1828. Wren's design for St Paul's Cathedral, the so-called Great Model of 1673–4, was constructed ten years after his first architectural commission in 1663. Faraday demonstrated the electromagnetic principles of the motor and the dynamo in 1821, a decade after he began studying science in 1810. Kekulé's theory of the benzene ring was published in 1865, about ten years after his first dream of his structural theory on a London omnibus. Pauling's quantum-mechanical theory of the chemical bond was published in 1931, ten years after he started to study the problem at university in 1920–1. Berners-Lee invented the World Wide Web in 1990, ten years after his first web-like computer programme. It is not difficult to multiply examples.

The arts frequently show the rule in operation, too. Percy Bysshe Shelley's creative explosion of 1819–20 (*The Mask of Anarchy*, *Prometheus Unbound*, and other works) occurred ten years after he wrote and published his first poetry and fiction in 1809–10. Ernest Hemingway's *The Sun Also Rises* was written in 1925–6, ten years after he began publishing fiction and journalism in his school magazine. Picasso's *Les Demoiselles d'Avignon* was painted in 1907, a decade after he began training as an artist in Barcelona in 1896. Henri de Toulouse-Lautrec's *At the Moulin Rouge* was painted in 1892, ten years after he entered the atelier of his first art teacher in 1882. Satyajit Ray's first film, *Pather Panchali*, was completed in 1955, a decade after he created woodcuts to illustrate an edition of the original novel in 1944 and began writing scenarios. Igor Stravinsky's *The Rite of Spring* was composed in 1912, ten years after he began his apprenticeship to Nikolai Rimsky-Korsakov in 1902. Even The Beatles seem to obey the rule: they composed *Sergeant Pepper's Lonely Hearts Club Band* in 1967, ten years after John Lennon started playing with Paul McCartney in 1957.

In my view, the ten-year rule is best considered in three versions: weak, medium, and strong. (Even physicists sometimes use such distinctions.) The *weak* version is that a breakthrough requires a minimum of ten years' hard work and practice in a relevant domain – and it may take much longer. The *medium* version is more restrictive: a breakthrough requires a minimum of ten years' hard work and practice focused on the particular problem solved by the breakthrough. The *strong* version is more restrictive still: a breakthrough requires about ten years – no fewer and no more – of hard work and practice focused on the particular problem solved by the breakthrough. Of course, there are many exceptions to the strong version of the ten-year rule. However, exceptions to the weak version of the rule – in which a scientist or artist makes a breakthrough after *fewer* than ten years of hard work and practice in a domain – are extremely rare. Neither Einstein nor Mozart fits this last bill, despite our natural expectations of such prodigies.

Hayes discovered only three exceptions among classical composers, none of whom is in the top rank: Erik Satie composed a masterwork in year eight of his career, whilst Niccolò Paganini and Dmitry Shostakovich composed one masterwork each in year nine of their careers. A 'masterwork' was defined by Hayes as a work for which five different recordings were available in a leading music guide; by this definition, Mozart's first masterwork, the piano concerto No. 9, K271, appeared in year twelve of his career.

In the visual arts, Van Gogh painted some of his classic works in 1888 only eight years after beginning to paint; but he had earlier spent six or seven years working for an art dealer in the Hague, London, and Paris where he was in daily contact with masterpieces that had trained his eye and aroused his sensibility, so Van Gogh certainly did not start painting from square one in

**14. Portrait of Isaac Newton by Sir Godfrey Kneller, 1689. Newton was one of the tiny handful of geniuses to achieve a breakthrough in fewer than ten years**

1880. In the sciences, the theoretical physicist Werner Heisenberg, one of the pioneers of quantum theory, created matrix mechanics in 1925, aged 23, only about five years after beginning his university study of physics; but Heisenberg had two leading physicists, Max Born and Niels Bohr, as very close mentors during this period. Paul Dirac, another great theoretical physicist, may provide another exception: in 1928, he formulated the relativistic theory of the electron from which he predicted the existence of the positron, aged 25, about six years after beginning his university training in applied mathematics; but Dirac had previously taken a three-year degree in electrical engineering. Perhaps only Newton fairly and squarely beats the ten-year rule in science: his *annus mirabilis*, 1665–6, occurred after fewer than five years of solitary study at Cambridge, at the age of only 22/23.

The predominance of theoretical physics among the handful of exceptions may be a small clue to the explanation of the ten-year rule in exceptional creativity. In theoretical physics, years of laboratory grind are not required, nor are any of the corpus of facts about nature that have to be memorized and assimilated in other sciences, such as engineering, chemistry, geology, and biology. So the theoretical physicist needs to expend less time in perspiration than other scientists before he or she can reach the frontier of the subject and perhaps make a breakthrough. Indeed, the ten-year rule seems to me to be an empirical truth about perspiration and inspiration equivalent to that of Edison's personal guess – not only in its underlying rationale but also approximately in its ratio. Instead of Edison's 'ninety-nine per cent versus one per cent' estimate, for every ten years (120 months) of hard work, an individual may be granted, so to speak, a month or two's worth (one per cent) of 'sudden inspiration'. Discouraging as this may be, in one sense, it also means that hardly any genius in history – not even Darwin, Einstein, Leonardo, or Mozart – has been permitted to short-cut the long and gradual path to a creative breakthrough.

# Chapter 10
# Genius and us

Anyone older than a teenager knows that fashion is fickle, fame is transitory, and reputations rise and fall. In literature, many of the winners of the Nobel prize for literature, inaugurated in 1901, are now forgotten writers, even in their original languages. Who bothers to read the Nobel laureates Sully Prudhomme (1901), Carl Verner von Heidenstam (1915), Grazia Deledda (1926), or Pearl Buck (1938), for example? 'Every era exalts works that, in a few generations, prove to be period pieces', the literary critic Harold Bloom wrote in 2002 in *Genius: A Mosaic of One Hundred Exemplary Creative Minds*. 'With only a double or triple handful of exceptions, everything we now freshly acclaim is a potential antique, and antiques made out of language wind up in dustbins, and not in auction houses or museums.'

In classical music, two centuries after his birth in 1809, Mendelssohn's star is rising, by contrast. As J. S. Bach was once considered old-fashioned and churchy, so Mendelssohn has tended to be considered a facile Romantic. He occupied a middling rank in 20th-century surveys of composers. 'It is only recently that Mendelssohn has made the transition from being an "easy" composer to being a "composer with problems"', writes the veteran conductor and musicologist Christopher Hogwood in a foreword to *Mendelssohn in Performance*, a volume of essays by eleven different scholars that appeared in 2008. Other recent published scholarship on Mendelssohn involves the greater availability of his correspondence, several biographical studies, and critically scrutinized editions of many of his major works. The long-term results of all this labour by experts are still unclear. Conceivably, Mendelssohn's reputation will eventually rise to a level of genius close to that of Bach, Mozart, and Beethoven, where Hogwood and some other musicians believe it properly belongs.

In the visual arts, the ephemerality of reputation is especially evident. Some of the old masters, such as Titian, have waxed and waned in reputation with extraordinary rapidity. In a discourse in 1771, and after, the painter Joshua Reynolds, president of the Royal Academy of Arts, dismissed Italian painters such as Titian, Veronese, and Tintoretto as 'mere decorators, obsessed with colour at the expense of form': propaganda that had the effect of debasing the market for the 16th-century Venetian school of painting well into the 19th century, and raising the price of works by the 17th-century Italian masters owned by Reynolds's patrons, as he had intended.

Among the modern masters, Picasso's reputation is extremely high, but there is sound reason to question if this will last. Picasso himself expressed doubts about the value of much of his oeuvre, hinting that he had created it only to satisfy the demands of art dealers and the public. Even during his lifetime, high prices were paid only for his more realistic works, with the highest prices reserved for those painted in his twenties – a trend that has become more pronounced since the artist's death in his nineties in 1973, as mentioned earlier. The leading critic David Sylvester, despite his deep interest in 20th-century art, judged that none of its leading artists – he named Picasso, Matisse, and Piet Mondrian, in particular – was 'the equal of the great old masters'; Sylvester regarded Cézanne as 'the last of the pantheon'. The psychologist Colin Martindale, in his treatise attempting to find artistic 'laws' in creative trends over the centuries, *The Clockwork*

*Muse: The Predictability of Artistic Change*, suggests that if the past is any guide, Picasso's paintings may, 'at some point in the future, . . . be seen as so ugly, and their value will be so low, that no one will want them'. While Martindale's deliberately provocative view is not credible, a future aesthetic downgrading of Picasso from his Olympian dominance appears more than probable during the century after his death.

It is sobering to realize that less than half of the modern and contemporary artists listed a quarter of a century ago in the contemporary art catalogues of the biggest auction houses are still offered at any major auction. Not many people now know the name of the Czech-German painter Jiri George Dokoupil, for example, who in 1988 was ranked at 30 on the *Kunstkompass* (Art Compass) scale of top international artists, which is calculated from data such as exhibitions at major institutions and reviews in art magazines.

Some artists' reputations rise, fall, and rise again. Titian is an obvious example, as is Rembrandt, who enjoyed three short waves of great popularity prior to his present high estimation: in England during the Napoleonic Wars, in Germany and America in the 1870s and 1880s, and universally in the first 30 years of the 20th century. An intriguing example is the rise, fall, and rise of the Dutch-born Lawrence Alma-Tadema – possibly the most successful painter of the Victorian era. Alma-Tadema specialized in lush history painting of the ancient world, and was a stickler for accuracy based on his detailed archaeological and architectural research. Settling in London, he was quickly elected a Royal Academician, and in due course was not only knighted but also created a member of the exclusive Order of Merit, established by King Edward VII in 1902 – despite his having been derided by the critic John Ruskin as the worst painter of the 19th century. The year after his death in 1912, there was a tremendous memorial exhibition of all of Alma-Tadema's paintings at the Royal Academy.

In 1888, Alma-Tadema began one of his most celebrated works, *The Roses of Heliogabalus*, depicting an episode from the scandalous life of the Roman emperor Heliogabalus in which the emperor arranged to smother a party of his unsuspecting guests to death with rose-petals released from false ceiling panels. For four months in 1888, roses were sent daily from the French Riviera to Alma-Tadema's studio during a London winter, in order to ensure the correctness of each petal in the painting. The work was commissioned for the exorbitant sum of £4,000 (at 1888 prices). A second famous painting, this time on a biblical theme, *The Finding of Moses*, was commissioned for £5,250 in 1904. Yet, at a major art auction in 1960, *The Roses of Heliogabalus* fetched a mere £105, and *The Finding of Moses* commanded a price of just £252. By mid-century, half a century after his death, Alma-Tadema did not rate a mention in general histories of painting, such as Ernst Gombrich's *The Story of Art*. Nor is he once referred to in a current history of the Royal Academy, *School of Genius* by James Fenton.

During the second half of the century, however, a cult of Alma-Tadema gradually got going. In 1995, *The Finding of Moses* set a new auction record of $2.8 million in New York. The main reason seems to have been that Alma-Tadema's meticulous, gorgeous, if lacklustre, recreations of scenes from antiquity caught the attention of Hollywood film-makers during the 20th century, as they had the eye of moneyed Victorians. The Hollywood remake of *The Ten Commandments* in 1956 by Cecil B. DeMille used prints of Alma-Tadema paintings to aid its set designs. In 2000, they were a key source of inspiration for *Gladiator*, an Oscar-winning Roman epic. Much as many of us may like to mock Alma-Tadema – as Ruskin first did – his sentimental, sometimes mildly pornographic, tableaux of Victorians dressed as ancient Greeks and Romans cannot be entirely ignored. Indeed, this fêted 19th-century painter of classical scenes enjoys a kind of kitsch celebrity in the early 21st century, even though no serious art critic would dream of ranking Alma-Tadema as a genius.

With some other minor artists, a single work can catch and retain the attention of the public, even though no other works by the artist are remembered. Galenson terms this phenomenon – which is also found in literature and music – 'masterpieces without masters'. Examples in the visual arts are: the sexually charged, Surrealist cup, saucer, and spoon covered in gazelle fur, known as *Le Déjeuner en fourrure (Luncheon in Fur)*, made by Meret Oppenheim in 1936; the Pop Art collage satirizing the upcoming consumer society, *Just what is it that makes today's homes so different, so appealing?*, created by Richard Hamilton in 1956; and the Vietnam Veterans Memorial in Washington DC, two long walls of polished black granite arranged in a V shape, designed by Maya Lin in 1982. Again, no critic would be tempted to call Oppenheim, Hamilton, or Lin a genius; and yet each of these three works is reproduced so often that they enjoy an iconic status comparable with the best-known works of recognized masters.

Although fashion, swings in expert opinion, celebrity, and social movements are especially influential on reputation in the arts, they can also apply to some extent in the sciences. During the early 19th century, the chemist Sir Humphry Davy – discoverer of nitrous oxide (laughing gas) and of many chemical elements such as sodium and potassium, inventor of the miner's safety lamp, a sought-after and effervescent lecturer, a friend of the powerful, and president of the Royal Society from 1820 to 1827 – was Britain's most famous living scientist, whose Royal Institution assistant was the humble young Michael Faraday. Some two centuries later, Davy, unlike Faraday, is not much remembered and his scientific work, though undoubtedly significant in its time, is a period piece studied only by historians of science – in contrast to that of his predecessor Newton, his successor Darwin, and even his far less fashionable immediate contemporary at the Royal Institution and the Royal Society, Thomas Young. In today's world, the fact that Stephen Hawking is perhaps the only living scientist who is a household name like Curie, Darwin, and Einstein undoubtedly has much to do with

Hawking's much-publicized triumph over his disability, his bestselling book, *A Brief History of Time*, and the mind-boggling nature of cosmology.

Though eligible for a Nobel prize as a physicist (despite being a professor of mathematics), Hawking has not been awarded one. Are the Nobel prizes a corrective to fashion, fame, and celebrity – a true record of genius born in the 19th and 20th centuries, as their founder Alfred Nobel, who detested celebrity, hoped for in his will? Certainly, Nobel prizes neither reward, nor confer, celebrity: very few of us can name from memory all, or most, of the previous few years' Nobel prize winners, even in the widely accessible fields of literature and peace. Very likely, the prizes bolster the concept of genius, by creating a seemingly magic circle of winners, and excluding the vast majority of workers in the field, however eminent they may be. Probably, the prizes fulfil their purpose well in the sciences, though much less well in literature, peace, and economics. In *The Nobel Prize: A History of Genius, Controversy, and Prestige*, Burton Feldman accurately remarks that:

> the science juries have long chosen far more impressive laureates than have the literary judges. Planck, Rutherford, Einstein, Bohr, Heisenberg, Dirac, Pauling, Crick and Watson, Feynman – a steady procession of greatness or the nearest equivalent. Would the Nobel have much of an aura or any at all without these names? The literature prizes, after 50 years of ignoring the likes of Leo Tolstoy, Bertolt Brecht, James Joyce, and Virginia Woolf, can never catch up with the prestige of the science lists. The prizes in literature, peace, and economics are not unlike pale fires, shining more brightly in the reflected light of Einstein and company.

Indeed, there have been calls for the economics prize, started only in 1968 by the Central Bank of Sweden and therefore not officially a Nobel prize, to be abolished, including several calls from past winners of the prize.

The literature prize has been adversely affected by several difficulties. In his will of 1896, Nobel directed that the prize be given for 'distinguished work of an idealistic tendency'. This phrase was initially interpreted by the judges of the Swedish Academy to rule out of consideration many great writers such as Henrik Ibsen, Tolstoy, and Émile Zola, though the interpretation of 'idealistic' was later changed, giving the prize a record after the Second World War much more impressive than in its first half-century. Then there is the lack of sufficient expertise in languages among the judges, so that their decision is based partly on reading a writer's work in translation rather than in its original language (the case with the first Asian Nobel prize, for Tagore, who wrote chiefly in Bengali but was judged on his English translations). As the circle of literatures under consideration has gradually widened beyond the major European languages to include the languages of Asia and Africa, this linguistic barrier has become almost insuperable. Most importantly of all, writers take time, sometimes decades, to establish themselves; and their reputations can take still longer to grow. The temptation for the Nobel judges is to wait until a writer is old and long past the period of his or her best work; inevitably, death sometimes intervenes before the prize can be awarded, as happened with Marcel Proust, Rainer Maria Rilke, and D. H. Lawrence.

The science prizes do not suffer from these difficulties. For the most part, original scientific theories and key experiments are recognized as such by the scientific community within a decade or two. Moreover, the prizes are frequently shared between two or a maximum of three winners (which still entails difficult and sometimes controversial judgements about whom to exclude). Nonetheless, there can be long gaps between the date of an original scientific achievement and its Nobel recognition. The Nobel physics committee resisted giving Einstein a prize for over a decade, and eventually awarded him the prize for 1921, not for his 1905 relativity theory, which was considered too controversial, but for quite different theoretical work on quantum theory that other scientists had proved in the laboratory. The astrophysicist Subrahmanyan Chandrasekhar had to wait half a century before receiving his prize in 1983 for work he had done in 1934.

Large swathes of intellectual activity are of course ineligible for a Nobel prize (as are music, painting and sculpture, the performing

15. *Einstein Lived Here*, cartoon by Herblock, first published in an American newspaper on the death of Einstein, 1955. (Copyright by the Herb Block Foundation)

arts, and cinema). Biology and mathematics are excluded, so are philosophy, psychology, social science, political science, and history. While this is obviously the consequence of Alfred Nobel's personal choice in his will, it is also a reflection of the difficulty of judging 'genius' in some of these fields. Not a few leading thinkers have proved fruitful for the advancement of knowledge, despite their ideas being wrong. This is true of some aspects of Darwin's biology, many aspects of Karl Marx's political thinking, and perhaps most of Freud's theory of psychoanalysis. Yet, the philosopher Isaiah Berlin wrote of Marx's theory of history and society: 'Even if all its specific conclusions were proved false, its importance in creating a wholly new attitude to social and historical questions, and so opening new avenues of human knowledge, would be unimpaired.' And the psychiatrist Anthony Storr said similarly of Freud: 'Even if every idea which Freud put forward could be proven wrong, we should still be greatly in his debt...He did cause a revolution in the way we think.' If Berlin and Storr are right, then it is at least arguable that Marx and Freud should each be regarded as a genius, as Darwin is.

In the early 21st century, talent appears to be on the increase, genius on the decrease. More scientists, writers, composers, and artists than ever before earn a living from their creative output. During the 20th century, performance standards and records continually improved in all fields – from music and singing to chess and sports. But where is the Darwin or the Einstein, the Mozart or the Beethoven, the Chekhov or the Shaw, the Cézanne or the Picasso or the Cartier-Bresson of today? In the cinema, the youngest of the arts, there is a growing feeling that the giants – directors such as Charles Chaplin, Akira Kurosawa, Satyajit Ray, Jean Renoir, and Orson Welles – have departed the scene, leaving behind the merely talented. Even in popular music, genius of the quality of Louis Armstrong, The Beatles, or Jimi Hendrix, seems to be a thing of the past. Of course, it may be that the geniuses of our time have yet to be recognized – a process that can take many decades after their deaths, as we know – but sadly, this seems unlikely, at least to me (though others will no doubt disagree), for reasons I shall now briefly explain.

In saying this, I know I am in danger of falling into a mindset mentioned by the great 19th-century South American explorer and polymath Alexander von Humboldt, 'the Albert Einstein of his day' (writes a recent biographer), in volume two of his five-volume survey *Cosmos*. 'Weak minds complacently believe that in their own age humanity has reached the culminating point of intellectual progress,' wrote Humboldt in the middle of the century, 'forgetting that by the internal connection existing among all the natural phenomena, in proportion as we advance, the field to be traversed acquires additional extension, and that it is bounded by a horizon which incessantly recedes before the eyes of the inquirer.' Humboldt was right. But his explorer's image surely also implies that as knowledge continues to advance, an individual will have the time to investigate a smaller and smaller proportion of the horizon with each passing generation, because the field will continually expand. So, if 'genius' requires breadth of knowledge, a synoptic vision – as it seems to – then it would appear to become harder to achieve as knowledge advances.

The ever-increasing professionalization and specialization of education and domains, especially in the sciences, is undeniable. The breadth of experience that feeds genius is harder to achieve today than in the 19th century, if not downright impossible. Had Darwin been required to do a PhD in the biology of barnacles, and then joined a university life sciences department, it is difficult to imagine his having the varied experiences and exposure to different disciplines that led to his discovery of natural selection. If the teenaged Van Gogh had gone straight to an art academy in Paris, instead of spending years working for an art dealer, trying to become a pastor, and self-tutoring himself in art while dwelling among poor Dutch peasants, would we have his late efflorescence of great painting? A second reason for the diminution of genius appears to be the ever-increasing commercialization of the arts (manifested in the cult of celebrity). True originality takes time – at least ten years – to come to fruition; and the results may well take further time to find their audience and market. Few beginning artists, or scientists, will be fortunate enough to enjoy financial support, like Van Gogh or Darwin, over such an extended period. It is much less challenging, and more remunerative, to make a career by producing imitative, sensational, or repetitive work, like Alma-Tadema, Warhol, or any number of professional scientists who, as Einstein remarked, 'take a board of wood, look for its thinnest part, and drill a great number of holes when the drilling is easy'. Thirdly, if less obviously, our expectations of modern genius have become more sophisticated and discriminating since the time of the 19th-century Romantic movement, partly as a result of 20th-century advances in psychology and psychiatry. The 'long hair, great black hats, capes, and cloaks' of the bona-fide Victorian hero, ironically mentioned by Virginia Woolf, are now period pieces, concealing psychological complexes more than genius.

There is also the anti-elitist *Zeitgeist* to consider. Genius is an idea that invites attack by scientific sceptics and cultural levellers. In 1986, Robert Weisberg published a short and readable book with the title *Creativity: Beyond the Myth of Genius: What You, Mozart, Einstein, and Picasso Have in Common*. Perhaps the second subtitle was chosen by the hopeful publisher (who reprinted the book in 1993), rather than the author. At any rate, it encapsulates a widespread desire to vaunt genius whilst simultaneously cutting it down to normal size. A cartoon strip published in *Scientific American* during the centenary of Einstein's 1905 breakthroughs parodied this paradox with a sketch of a book called *The Einstein Diet* captioned: 'What did this mega-genius eat? Read this book and unlock Albert's diet secrets.' A snip at $84.99.

Genius is not a myth, and it is worthy of our aspirations. But it comes at a cost to the individual – expressed in the ten-year rule – that most of us are unable or unwilling to pay. There are no short-cuts to becoming a genius. The breakthroughs achieved by geniuses did not involve magic or miracles. They were the work of human grit, not the product of superhuman grace. From this truth about genius, we can surely derive both strength and stimulus for our own life and work – if we sincerely desire to.

# Further reading

## Chapter 1: Defining genius

E. T. Bell, *Men of Mathematics* (London: Victor Gollancz, 1937)

Daniel Coyle, *The Talent Code* (London: Random House, 2009)

H. J. Eysenck, *Genius: The Natural History of Creativity* (Cambridge: Cambridge University Press, 1995)

Francis Galton, *Hereditary Genius: An Inquiry into Its Laws and Consequences* (Amherst: Prometheus, 2006)

M. J. A. Howe, J. W. Davidson, and J. A. Sloboda, 'Innate Talents: Reality or Myth?', *Behavioral and Brain Sciences*, 21 (1998): 399–442

Penelope Murray (ed.), *Genius: The History of an Idea* (Oxford: Blackwell, 1989)

Andrew Steptoe, 'Mozart: Resilience Under Stress', in *Genius and the Mind: Studies of Creativity and Temperament*, ed. Andrew Steptoe (Oxford: Oxford University Press, 1998)

## Chapter 2: Family affairs

Mihaly Csikszentmihalyi, *Creativity: Flow and the Psychology of Discovery and Invention* (New York: HarperCollins, 1996)

Victor Goertzel and Mildred Goertzel, *Cradles of Eminence* (London: Constable, 1962)

R. Ochse, *Before the Gates of Excellence: The Determinants of Creative Genius* (Cambridge: Cambridge University Press, 1990)

## Chapter 3 : The schooling of genius

Robert Kanigel, *The Man Who Knew Infinity: A Life of the Genius Ramanujan* (London: Scribners, 1991)

Andrew Robinson, *The Man Who Deciphered Linear B: The Story of Michael Ventris* (London: Thames & Hudson, 2002)

Dean Keith Simonton, *Genius, Creativity and Leadership: Historiometric Inquiries* (Cambridge, Mass.: Harvard University Press, 1984)

John Tusa, *On Creativity: Interviews Exploring the Process* (London: Methuen, 2003)

## Chapter 4: Intelligence and creativity

Catharine M. Cox, *The Early Mental Traits of Three Hundred Geniuses*, vol. 2 of *Genetic Studies of Genius*, ed. L. M. Terman (Stanford: Stanford University Press, 1926)

James R. Flynn, *What Is Intelligence?: Beyond the Flynn Effect* (Cambridge: Cambridge University Press, 2007)

David Lubinski and Camilla Persson Benbow, 'Study of Mathematically Precocious Youth After 35 Years: Uncovering Antecedents for the Development of Math-Science Expertise', *Perspectives on Psychological Science*, 1 (2006): 316–45

Robert J. Sternberg (ed.), *Handbook of Creativity* (Cambridge: Cambridge University Press, 1999)

L. M. Terman, 'Psychological Approaches to the Biography of Genius', in *Creativity: Selected Readings*, ed. P. E. Vernon (London: Penguin, 1970)

## Chapter 5 : Genius and madness

Nancy C. Andreasen, *The Creating Brain: The Neuroscience of Genius* (New York: Dana Press, 2005)

Richard M. Berlin (ed.), *Poets on Prozac: Mental Illness, Treatment and the Creative Process* (Baltimore: Johns Hopkins University Press, 2008)

Noel L. Brann, *The Debate over the Origin of Genius during the Italian Renaissance: The Theories of Supernatural Frenzy and Natural Melancholy in Accord and in Conflict on the Threshold of the Scientific Revolution* (Leiden: Brill, 2002)

Genius

Kay Redfield Jamison, *Touched with Fire: Manic-Depressive Illness and the Artistic Temperament* (New York: Free Press, 1994)

Royal Academy of Arts (no ed.), *The Real Van Gogh: The Artist and His Letters* (London: Royal Academy of Arts, 2010)

Andrew Steptoe, 'Artistic Temperament in the Italian Renaissance: A Study of Giorgio Vasari's *Lives*', in *Genius and the Mind: Studies of Creativity and Temperament*, ed. Andrew Steptoe (Oxford: Oxford University Press, 1998)

## Chapter 6 : Chameleon personalities

Banesh Hoffmann, *Albert Einstein: Creator and Rebel* (New York: Viking, 1972)

Daniel Nettle, *Personality: What Makes You the Way You Are* (Oxford: Oxford University Press, 2007)

Robert W. Weisberg, *Creativity: Understanding Innovation in Problem Solving, Science, Invention, and the Arts* (Hoboken: John Wiley, 2006)

## Chapter 7: Arts versus sciences

Peter Medawar, *Pluto's Republic* (Oxford: Oxford University Press, 1982)

Dean Keith Simonton, *Creativity in Science: Chance, Logic, Genius, and Zeitgeist* (Cambridge: Cambridge University Press, 2004)

C. P. Snow, *The Two Cultures: and A Second Look* (Cambridge: Cambridge University Press, 1964)

Gunther S. Stent, 'Meaning in Art and Science', in *The Origins of Creativity*, ed. Karl H. Pfenninger and Valerie R. Shubik (New York: Oxford University Press, 2001)

## Chapter 8: Eureka experiences

Frederic Lawrence Holmes, *Investigative Pathways: Patterns and Stages in the Careers of Experimental Scientists* (Newhaven: Yale University Press, 2004)

David Perkins, *The Eureka Effect: The Art and Logic of Breakthrough Thinking* (New York: Norton, 2000)

Andrew Robinson, *Writing and Script: A Very Short Introduction* (Oxford: Oxford University Press, 2009)

Alan J. Rocke, 'Hypothesis and Experiment in the Early Development of Kekulé's Benzene Theory', *Annals of Science*, 42 (1985): 355–81

## Chapter 9 : Perspiration and inspiration

David W. Galenson, *Old Masters and Young Geniuses: The Two Life Cycles of Artistic Creativity* (Princeton: Princeton University Press, 2008)

Howard Gardner, *Creating Minds: An Anatomy of Creativity Seen Through the Lives of Freud, Einstein, Picasso, Stravinsky, Eliot, Graham, and Gandhi* (New York: Basic Books, 1993)

J. R. Hayes, 'Cognitive Processes in Creativity', in *Handbook of Creativity*, ed. J. A. Glover, R. R. Ronning, and C. R. Reynolds (New York: Plenum, 1989)

Arthur Koestler, *The Act of Creation* (London: Hutchinson, 1964)

## Chapter 10 : Genius and us

Harold Bloom, *Genius: A Mosaic of One Hundred Exemplary Creative Minds* (London: Fourth Estate, 2002)

Leo Braudy, *The Frenzy of Renown: Fame and Its History* (New York: Vintage, 1997)

Robert Currie, *Genius: An Ideology in Literature* (London: Chatto & Windus, 1974)

Burton Feldman, *The Nobel Prize: A History of Genius, Controversy, and Prestige* (New York: Arcade, 2000)

Colin Martindale, *The Clockwork Muse: The Predictability of Artistic Change* (New York: Basic Books, 1990)

Gerald Reitlinger, *The Economics of Taste: The Rise and Fall of Picture Prices 1760–1960* (London: Barrie and Rockcliff, 1961)

Aaron Sachs, *The Humboldt Current: A European Explorer and His American Disciples* (Oxford: Oxford University Press, 2007)

# Index

Index

# INTELLIGENCE
## A Very Short Introduction
Ian J. Deary

Ian J. Deary takes readers with no knowledge about the science of human intelligence to a stage where they can make informed judgements about some of the key questions about human mental activities. He discusses different types of intelligence, and what we know about how genes and the environment combine to cause these differences; he addresses their biological basis, and whether intelligence declines or increases as we grow older. He charts the discoveries that psychologists have made about how and why we vary in important aspects of our thinking powers.

'There has been no short, up to date and accurate book on the science of intelligence for many years now. This is that missing book. Deary's informal, story-telling style will engage readers, but it does not in any way compromise the scientific seriousness of the book . . . excellent.'

**Linda Gottfredson, University of Delaware**

'Ian Deary is a world-class leader in research on intelligence and he has written a world-class introduction to the field . . . This is a marvellous introduction to an exciting area of research.'

**Robert Plomin, University of London**

www.oup.co.uk/isbn/0-19-289321-1

# LOGIC
## A Very Short Introduction
### Graham Priest

Logic is often perceived as an esoteric subject, having little to do with the rest of philosophy, and even less to do with real life. In this lively and accessible introduction, Graham Priest shows how wrong this conception is. He explores the philosophical roots of the subject, explaining how modern formal logic deals with issues ranging from the existence of God and the reality of time to paradoxes of self-reference, change, and probability. Along the way, the book explains the basic ideas of formal logic in simple, non-technical terms, as well as the philosophical pressures to which these have responded. This is a book for anyone who has ever been puzzled by a piece of reasoning.

> 'a delightful and engaging introduction to the basic concepts of logic. Whilst not shirking the problems, Priest always manages to keep his discussion accessible and instructive.'
>
> **Adrian Moore, St Hugh's College, Oxford**

> 'an excellent way to whet the appetite for logic. . . . Even if you read no other book on modern logic but this one, you will come away with a deeper and broader grasp of the *raison d'être* for logic.'
>
> **Chris Mortensen, University of Adelaide**

www.oup.co.uk/isbn/0-19-289320-3

# DARWIN
## A Very Short Introduction
Jonathan Howard

Darwin's theory of evolution, which implied that our ancestors were apes, caused a furore in the scientific world and beyond when *The Origin of Species* was published in 1859. Arguments still rage about the implications of his evolutionary theory, and scepticism about the value of Darwin's contribution to knowledge is widespread. In this analysis of Darwin's major insights and arguments, Jonathan Howard reasserts the importance of Darwin's work for the development of modern science and culture.

'Jonathan Howard has produced an intellectual *tour de force*, a classic in the genre of popular scientific exposition which will still be read in fifty years' time'

**Times Literary Supplement**

www.oup.co.uk/isbn/0-19-285454-2

# ONLINE CATALOGUE
## A Very Short Introduction

Our online catalogue is designed to make it easy to find your ideal Very Short Introduction. View the entire collection by subject area, watch author videos, read sample chapters, and download reading guides.

# SOCIAL MEDIA
## Very Short Introduction

# Join our community
www.oup.com/vsi

- Join us online at the official Very Short Introductions **Facebook** page.
- Access the thoughts and musings of our authors with our online **blog**.
- Sign up for our monthly **e-newsletter** to receive information on all new titles publishing that month.
- Browse the full range of Very Short Introductions online.
- Read **extracts** from the Introductions for free.
- Visit our library of **Reading Guides**. These guides, written by our expert authors will help you to question again, why you think what you think.
- If you are a teacher or lecturer you can order inspection copies quickly and simply via our website.